# Dreaming on a Sunday in the Alameda
# and Other Plays

Chicana & Chicano Visions of the Américas

# Chicana & Chicano Visions of the Américas

*Series Editor*
Robert Con Davis-Undiano

*Editorial Board*
Rudolfo Anaya
Denise Chávez
David Draper Clark
María Amparo Escandón
María Herrera-Sobek
Rolando Hinojosa-Smith
Demetria Martínez
Carlos Monsiváis
Rafael Pérez-Torres
Leroy V. Quintana
José Davíd Saldívar
Ramón Saldívar

# Dreaming on a Sunday in the Alameda and Other Plays

## Carlos Morton

*Introduction by María Herrera-Sobek*

UNIVERSITY OF OKLAHOMA PRESS : NORMAN

Also by Carlos Morton

*Rancho Hollywood y Otras Obras del Teatro Chicano* (Houston, 1999)
*Johnny Tenorio and Other Plays* (Houston, 1992)
*The Many Deaths of Danny Rosales and Other Plays* (Houston, 1983)

Library of Congress Cataloging-in-Publication Data

Morton, Carlos.
 Dreaming on a Sunday in the Alameda and other plays / Carlos
Morton ; introduction by María Herrera-Sobek.
  p.  cm. — (Chicana & Chicano visions of the Américas ; v. 3)
 Contents: La Malinche—Dreaming on a Sunday in the Alameda—
Esperanza.
  ISBN 0–8061–3626–X (alk. paper) — ISBN 0–8061–3641–3
(pbk. : alk. paper)
 1. Mexican Americans—Drama.  2. Mexico—Drama.  I. Title  II. Series

 PS3563.O88194D74 2004
 812'.54—dc 22

                                                    2004045870

*Dreaming on a Sunday in the Alameda* is Volume 3 in the Chicana &
Chicano Visions of the Américas series.

1  2  3  4  5  6  7  8  9  10

*I dedicate these three plays to my three sons,*
*Seth, Miguel, and Xuncu,*
*for their posterity.*

# Contents

# Illustrations

# Introduction

## Carlos Morton's New Plays: Politically Engaged Theater for the Twenty-first Century

### MARÍA HERRERA-SOBEK

The Chicano playwright Carlos Morton offers us in this splendid collection, *Dreaming on a Sunday in the Alameda,* three outstanding new plays that highlight his continued production of politically engaged Chicano theater in the twenty-first century. The literary texts in this volume are characterized by perceptive insights into the human condition and encompass both tragedy and comedy. Some of the plays simultaneously incite the audiences to laugh as well as reflect on metaphysical issues for, through laughter, Morton peels away the surface layers of inauthentic reality in order to expose both philosophical and political issues that provide us with a deeper understanding of life.

Morton's new work evidences strong ties to his previous theatrical productions. The Chicago-born playwright is not new to theater, having begun his career as early as 1970 while still an undergraduate student at the University of Texas, El Paso, where he was publishing plays in such journals as *El Grito* and *Tejidos. El jardín* (1974) and *El cuento de Pancho Diablo* (1976), two of his first plays published in the these journals, provide clues to his later work, since both are biting satires that use comedy to deconstruct iconic figures from the realm of the sacred. In this same decade, as a graduate student, he wrote *The Many Muertes de Richard Morales,* also published in *Tejidos* (1977). This play was given a new title and appeared in the award-winning anthology *The Many Deaths of Danny Rosales and Other Plays* in 1983, together with *Rancho Hollywood, Los Dorados,* and *El jardín.* The docudrama

*The Many Deaths of Danny Rosales* later won the New York Shakespeare Festival's Hispanic Playwrights Festival Award in 1986, attesting to the play's significance and high quality.

Morton continued his education in theater arts and received his Ph.D. in 1987 from the University of Texas, Austin. He likewise continued writing plays in the 1980s; his most outstanding play during this period was *Johnny Tenorio* (1988), later published in the anthology *Johnny Tenorio and Other Plays* (1992), which included *The Savior, The Miser of Mexico,* and *Pancho Diablo.* His plays are frequently produced on university campuses and at community centers, as well as at professional theaters; they have been performed on international stages in Mexico, Honduras, Spain, Germany, and France.

Although Morton's first love is the theater, he has been very involved in teaching playwriting and Chicano/a theater. He has taught at the University of Texas, El Paso; the University of California (UC), Berkeley; and at UC Riverside. Currently, he is the director of the Center for Chicano Studies at UC Santa Barbara, where he also teaches in the Dramatic Art Department.

Morton's first drama in the present collection, *La Malinche,* is a tragedy and pays homage to La Malinche, Hernán Cortés's Indian mistress, translator, and mother of his first child, Martín. Malinche (also known by her Spanish name, Doña Marina) has suffered Mexican history's scorn. Perceived as a traitor, her name has become an epithet, an insult for those who betray or sell out one's country to a foreign nation. To be a *malinchista* is to be a Benedict Arnold. Chicana scholars such as Adelaida del Castillo and Norma Alarcón, however, have vigorously questioned the ill-treatment history has heaped on this woman who, after all, was given to Cortés as a slave at the age of fifteen or twenty years old. She did not join Cortés's army of her own free will but was a victim of the indigenous patriarchal system as well as the Spanish one. Furthermore, she could not have betrayed her country because at that time she had no country, since she had been sold into slavery to the Mayans by her own people as a child.

The play begins at the point where Cortés is preparing to wed his Spanish bride, Catalina. Malinche, feeling jilted and rejected by him, is angry and promises to seek revenge and punish her ex-lover for his betrayal. She begins plotting with Cihuacoatl and La Llorona, two pre-Hispanic women, the former a goddess and the latter a historical Indian woman, both associated with the kidnapping and killing of children. Malinche devises a scheme whereby she pretends to accept Cortés's betrayal and pretends to be resigned to the upcoming wedding, but secretly she concocts a plan to kill Catalina on her wedding day. The plot involves the offering of two presents: a gold headdress and a dress, both of which are laced with deadly poison and are to be presented to her by Martín, Malinche's son by Cortés. When Catalina opens her wedding presents, she is astounded by the glittering gold dress and feathered headdress given to her by the child, who is instructed to leave immediately so as not be harmed by the poison. Cortés's bride puts the garments on her body and immediately feels the poison taking effect; she screams as she begins to burn and instantaneously explodes as she clings to her evil uncle, Bishop Lizárraga. Cortés, enraged at what has happened to his bride, pursues La Malinche in order to kill her; he soon finds her mourning her dead son since the young mestizo child has been murdered by La Llorona with the conquistador's own sword. The play ends with the recriminations both Cortés and Malinche are hurling at each other over the death of their son.

The drama brings together two powerful female figures from Mexico's colonial period: La Malinche and La Llorona (the "Weeping Woman," also linked to the Aztec goddess Cihuacoatl). Oftentimes, popular culture conflates the two, perceiving Malinche as La Llorona since the latter's story parallels Malinche's. According to legend, La Llorona was supposedly an indigenous or mestizo woman who fell in love with a Spaniard and had children by him. When he abandoned her to marry a Spanish woman, La Llorona, in a fit of rage and in order to punish his betrayal, murdered her own children. God punishes her, condemning her to forever roam rivers, lakes, forests, and waterways screaming "¡Aayyy mis hijos!" (Oh my children!).

The tragedy is presented from La Malinche's (and, by extension, the indigenous people's) perspective. The death of the child (representing the murdering of Native American people) was caused not by the mother but by the imperial, conquering sword of the invading country—Spain.

Morton's second play in this volume is based on Diego Rivera's famous mural *Dreaming on a Sunday in the Alameda*, from which the title of the play is derived. The mural is the point of departure for this play. Act 1 begins with Rivera conversing with his assistant, a Chicano painter named Johnny, while they are painting the mural on one of the walls of the Hotel El Prado, located across from the lovely and renowned Alameda Park in Mexico City. The various characters painted on the mural come to life, step out of the painting, and begin to interact with Rivera. The monk, representative of the Catholic Church, is the first to spar with Diego regarding the inconsistencies in the painter's ideological positions, that is, his negative stance toward capitalism but his involvement with capitalists painting murals for Nelson Rockefeller in New York and for Henry Ford in Detroit. Rivera counters with accusations of the church's maltreatment of the indigenous populations.

Frida Kahlo is the second character to step out from the mural. A history of the stormy relationship between the two is detailed through a series of dialogues. Rivera's womanizing is brought to task, and Frida's sexual relationships are also highlighted. Other important characters making appearances include Sor Juana Inés de la Cruz, Hernán Cortés, the Mexican dictator Porfirio Díaz, and La Catrina, representative of death. In the end, Rivera succumbs to an illness, and La Catrina is only too happy to take him away. The play is a vitriolic critique of a cross section of Mexican society. It is a splendid satire on the foibles of human beings, whether they are nuns, dictators, painters, or conquistadores. Morton's pen is unforgiving, although he laces his critique with a strong sense of humor.

The third entry included in this collection is titled *Esperanza*, described as an opera in two acts. The opera is adapted from the screenplay for *Salt of the Earth*, filmed in 1953 by the blacklisted director Herbert Biberman. The film depicts the struggle of impoverished mine workers for decent wages and safe working conditions. *Esperanza* is one of the first Chicano operas ever written and as such is a landmark in this ethnic group's literary production. It portrays the epic struggle of the miners from Zinc Town, New Mexico, against the Delaware Zinc Mining Company, which forces the miners to work long hours under unsafe and dangerous conditions for such meager pay that the earnings barely sustain them. These unsafe conditions are responsible for the injury of two workers and ignite the fuse that impels the miners to stage a strike against the mining company. The main protagonists are Esperanza and her husband, Ramón Quintero. The strikers, composed entirely of the male miners, begin their strike, but soon the Delaware Mining Company brings in the sheriff of Zinc County to harass the strikers and imprison them. Nevertheless, the miners persist in their strike until an injunction written under the Taft-Hartley Act prohibits them from picketing. Nevertheless, the miners' wives identify a loophole in the injunction, since the Taft-Hartley Act does not prohibit the women from picketing. A plot is hatched to allow the women to continue the picketing, but the community first has to decide by a vote whether to allow the women to picket the mines since some men, including Ramón, are firmly against it. The vote is taken, and it is in the affirmative; soon the women begin picketing the mine, and even though the sheriff and his cronies harass them, the women do not give up and persist in their picketing. Eventually, the mining company gives up and decides to settle with the miners.

The drama is structured in two parts: the struggle for social justice on the part of the miners and the struggle for equality on the part of the women. The male Chicanos feel oppressed, exploited, and discriminated against by Anglo-American hegemonic society. On the other hand, they are oblivious to the oppression, exploitation, and unequal treatment they give their own wives. While the issue regarding workers' rights predominates in act 1, act 2 focuses on the rights of women and Esperanza's struggle (representative of all women) to force Ramón, her husband, to acknowledge the asymmetrical relationship between men and women and the right to equality and self-determination for all concerned. Through the struggle for decent wages, both men and women become socially transformed; they acquire agency and become speaking subjects in charge of their own destiny.

Carlos Morton's three socially relevant and provocative plays engage key moments in Mexican and Mexican American history with contemporary political issues. The drama *La Malinche* reconceptualizes and re-visions the sixteenth-century historical figures of La Malinche and La Llorona in order to proffer a different perspective on this much-maligned figure. In Morton's play, La Malinche offers her child, Martín, to La Llorona to be sacrificed. This horrendous deed is done in an effort to prevent Cortés from transforming the boy into a Spaniard, since Malinche does not want her son to become an instrument of death and destruction against his own people in the future.

Likewise *Dreaming on a Sunday in the Alameda* deconstructs through humor iconic figures in history such as Diego Rivera, Frida Kahlo, Hernán Cortés, Porfirio Díaz, and Sor Juana Inés de la Cruz. Morton brings to task Rivera's womanizing as well as his hobnobbing with capitalist entrepreneurs while ideologically claiming to be a committed socialist on the side of the working class. The pompous nature of the Catholic Church is similarly deconstructed through the buffoonish figure of Sor Juana Inés and the hypocritical monk.

Finally, in *Esperanza*, Morton critiques labor and gender relations and expertly unmasks both capitalists and patriarchal systems that oppress men and women. Nevertheless, through the actions of the main protagonist, Esperanza, signifying and literally meaning hope, there is a note of optimism inscribed in the literary text for the future of both labor and gender issues.

The Chicano playwright's three masterpieces are a call for reflection on our ethical and moral values and the manner in which human beings treat each other. Through the use of comedy and tragedy, of the buffoonish and the sublime, of biting satire and political idealism, Morton enjoins us to imagine a better world for all humanity.

# Acknowledgments

The roots of this collection go back twenty years when I was a graduate student at the University of Texas, Austin. *La Malinche* was written in 1983, and Professors Webster Smalley, Coleman Jennings, and Amarante Lucero of the Drama Department helped in a workshop production of the play that was coproduced with the Center for Mexican American Studies.

*La Malinche* sat in a drawer fermenting for twelve years before I submitted it in 1995 to the Arizona Theatre Company's Hispanic Playwriting Contest. It won First Prize of $1,000 and a production in Genesis, their play development series. It was directed by William (Bill) Virchis, with Yareli Arizmendi in the staring role of La Malinche. The play went on to receive its world premiere at the Arizona Theatre Company (directed by Abel Lopez) as part of their 1997 season. I am especially grateful to Artistic Director David Ira Goldstein and Managing Director Jessica Andrews. That same year *La Malinche* was also produced at Rio Hondo College, Whittier, California, and directed by William Korf.

*Dreaming on a Sunday in the Alameda* (formerly *The Child Diego*) was written in Spanish while on a Fulbright at the National University of Mexico (UNAM) in 1989-90. I translated it into English thanks to a Creative Activities Grant from the University of California Institute on Mexico and the United States (UC MEXUS) several years later. It was further developed through staged readings at First Stage in Hollywood (Richard Hornby); Mascara Magica (Bill Virchis) in a Southern

California tour; Miracle Theatre in Portland, Oregon; and Borderlands Theatre in Tucson, Arizona. It received its premiere at the University of California (UC), Riverside in 1995 (directed by Eduardo Rodriguez Solís) and had a subsequent production at Arizona State University (directed by Daniel Irvine) in 1996.

*Esperanza* was commissioned by the State Historical Society of Wisconsin and the AFL-CIO of Wisconsin. Kathy McElroy was our guiding light and facilitator, bringing together the artistic team of Karlos Moser (conductor), David Bishop (composer), Norma Saldivar (stage director), and myself. The libretto had a staged reading at the Windmill Playwrights Festival in Lubbock, Texas, in 2000. The opera *Esperanza* premiered at the School of Music at the University of Wisconsin in 2000. It had a subsequent production by the Euterpe Opera Theater Company at the California Theatre for the Performing Arts in San Bernardino and UC Riverside in 2002, with Ruth Charloff conducting and Bill Virchis directing. For this production, a special thanks goes to Robert Nava of UC Riverside as well as to Tony Bocanegra and Frances Vasquez of the Sinfonia Mexicana.

For the manuscript preparation at UC Santa Barbara, I thank Leda Echevers and Karen Cisneros at the Center for Chicano Studies, as well as María Herrera-Sobek for agreeing to write the foreword. At the University of Oklahoma Press, Roberto C. Davis-Undiano selected the manuscript for inclusion in the Chicana & Chicano Visions of the Américas Series, and Karen C. Wieder guided me through the publication process.

I must also thank several lifelong collaborators. One is Jorge Huerta of UC San Diego, mentor, critic, and friend, who read all the plays, saw the productions, and has written extensively about my work. The other is my wife, Azalea Marin, who not only taught me Spanish but also the meaning of what it is to be Mexican.

CARLOS MORTON

# Performance History

## La Malinche

### Staged Reading

1995   Arizona Theatre Company, Tucson, Ariz.

### Productions

1984   University of Texas, Austin, Tex.
1997   Arizona Theatre Company, Tucson and Phoenix, Ariz.
1997   Rio Hondo College, Whittier, Calif.

## Dreaming on a Sunday in the Alameda (formerly The Child Diego)

### Staged Readings

1992   FIRST STAGE, Hollywood, Calif.
1992   Miracle Theatre, Portland, Oreg.
1992   University of California, Santa Barbara, Calif.
1992   University of California, Riverside, Calif.
1992   Centro Cultural de la Raza, San Diego, Calif.
1994   Borderlands Theatre, Tucson, Ariz.

## Productions

1995   Theatre Department, University of California, Riverside, Calif.
1996   Theatre Department, Arizona State University, Tempe, Ariz.

## *Esperanza: A Libretto for an Opera*

### Staged Reading

2000   Windmill Playwrights Festival, Lubbock, Tex.

### Productions

2000   School of Music, University of Wisconsin, Madison, Wisc.
2003   Euterpe Opera Theatre Company and Sinfonia Mexicana, California Theatre for the Performing Arts and University of California, Riverside, Calif.

# Dreaming on a Sunday in the Alameda and Other Plays

# La Malinche

# Characters

(In Order of Appearance)

LA LLORONA*: The "Weeping Woman," an Aztec goddess who carries an empty cradle, looking and lamenting for her lost children; also WOMAN

CIUACOATL: Servant and confidante of La Malinche

LA MALINCHE: Malintzin, also known as Doña Marina, mistress of Cortés

SÁNCHEZ: Spanish soldier under the command of Cortés; also SOLDIER

BISHOP LIZÁRRAGA: Head of the Catholic Church in New Spain; also PRIEST

HERNÁN CORTÉS: Captain general of New Spain

MARTÍN: Mestizo son of Malinche and Cortés, age seven (non-speaking role)

CATALINA: Cortés's Spanish wife-to-be (nonspeaking role)

---

*Note: Parts of LA LLORONA's speeches are inspired by traditional Aztec sources, such as the *Florentine Codex* and poetry by Nazahualcoyotal. Reference sources include Miguel León-Portilla's *The Broken Spears: The Aztec Account of the Conquest of Mexico*, translated by Lysander Kemp (Boston: Beacon Press, 1962); and Miguel León-Portilla's *Aztec Thought and Culture: A Study of the Ancient Nahuatl Mind*, translated by Jack Emory Davis (Norman: University of Oklahoma Press, 1963) 4th printing.

*The action begins shortly before dawn on a winter's day. Mist rises up from nearby Lake Texcoco. Enter an old woman dressed in long, flowing robes. She carries an empty cradle, rocking it as she sings the following lament.*

LLORONA

> Todos me dicen La Negra, Llorona
> Negra pero cariñosa
> Yo soy come el chile verde, Llorona,
> Picante pero sabrosa.
> Ay de mí, Llorona, Llorona
> Llorona de azul celeste
> Y aunque la vida me cueste, Llorona
> No dejaré de quererte.
> Dicen que no tienes duelo, Llorona
> Porque no te ven llorar
> Hay muertos que no hacen ruido, Llorona
> Y es más grande su penar.

*Enter CIUACOATL with a lantern partially revealing the front of LA MALINCHE's house in Tenochtitlan, Mexico.*

CIUACOATL

Old mother! Is it really you?

LLORONA

(*Embracing her.*) Ciuacoatl, my child!

CIUACOATL

Was that you I heard crying?

LLORONA

It was the hoot owls.

CIUACOATL

(*Bringing the lantern closer.*) There are tears in your eyes.

LLORONA

Like the fog hanging over the city.

CIUACOATL

It's been so long. What brings you back?

LLORONA

Malintzin calls out to me.

CIUACOATL

You heard then? Cortés betrayed my mistress! (*LA LLORONA nods her head solemnly.*) He is to marry a Spanish woman.

LLORONA

He has thrown away the fruit for the husk.

CIUACOATL

What will she do? What will happen to her and her son?

LLORONA

She seeks revenge.

CIUACOATL

I am afraid for her. She is capable of anything!

LLORONA

A raging river must run its course.

CIUACOATL

Her anguish is so great! (*A cry is heard from within the house.*) Listen!

LLORONA

(*They listen to MALINCHE's cries of anguish.*) Even from the depths of Mictlan, one hears her cries.

CIUACOATL

She has been like this for days, ever since she discovered Cortés will marry the bishop's niece.

LLORONA

When is the wedding to be?

CIUACOATL

The day after tomorrow! (*Enter LA MALINCHE.*) Look, there she is!

MALINCHE

¡Ay, mi hijo!

CIUACOATL

Do you hear her distress?

MALINCHE

Oh, my son, we must leave here . . . now!

CIUACOATL

At night she wanders the corridors . . . lost in the past.

MALINCHE

But where shall we go? Where will I take you?

LLORONA

In her mind, she goes through the steps that led her to this moment. (*Flutes and drums play. As LA LLORONA speaks, she conjures up the image of the Spaniards. LA LLORONA is the chorus that weaves the narrative. Enter CORTÉS, followed by a SOLDIER and a PRIEST.*) Can you see?

CIUACOATL

That was the first time we saw the bearded ones. Malintzin, myself, and a dozen other women were given to them as tribute.

LLORONA

Traitors were they to give their daughters and sisters to the enemy!

CIUACOATL

Sorrowful was the time the Spaniards entered my village in warm and verdant Yucatán. Sorrowful the day they took me and my mistress along on their cursed trail of conquest to the cold stones of Tenochtitlan.

MALINCHE

Why did I fall in love, Cortés
Was it your fame that preceded you?
We thought you a God
The reincarnation of Quetzalcoatl
Was it your beard, your horse, your cross, your sword?

(*A soldier approaches LA MALINCHE and tries to touch her, but she slaps his hand away. He grabs her by the arm, but she scratches his face, drawing blood.*)

SOLDIER

¡Bestia! (*Trying to strike her.*)

CORTÉS

(*Stepping in and stopping the SOLDIER from striking her.*) Come now, man, you are not going to get what you want by treating her that way! (*LA MALINCHE and CORTÉS are face to face.*)

LLORONA

(*To CIUACOATL.*) In that instant, something came over her, and she knew that her destiny would be forever entwined with his.

CORTÉS
Your name?

MALINCHE
Malintzin.

CORTÉS
(*Mispronouncing it.*) Mal-lin-che? They say you speak many languages.

LLORONA
Once Cortés discovered she spoke Nahuatl, the language of the Aztecs, her fate was sealed!

CORTÉS
(*Pointing to CIUACOATL.*) Soldier, take that one instead!

SOLDIER
(*Pointing to LA MALINCHE.*) But I want her!

CORTÉS
But her tongue is her most valuable asset, fool! (*Aside to the PRIEST.*) Make him listen to reason.

PRIEST
(*Stepping in before the SOLDIER can lead MALINCHE away.*) Soldier, stop!

SOLDIER
Why?

PRIEST
Well, they are unclean. These women have not been baptized.

SOLDIER
Well then! Do your duty, priest, baptize them!

PRIEST
What Christian name shall I give to this one? (*Pointing to LA MALINCHE.*)

CORTÉS
Ma-lin-che shall be . . . Marina. From now on she will be known as Marina.

PRIEST
(*Sprinkling her with water.*) I baptize you in the name of the Father, and of the Son, and of the Holy Ghost. (*LA LLORONA ends the*

*vision of the past. Exit LA LLORONA, MALINCHE, CORTÉS, SOLDIER, and PRIEST.*)

CIUACOATL

I never understood, arguing about saving souls, then giving her as a concubine to a common soldier.

SÁNCHEZ

(*Entering with a lantern and startling CIUACOATL.*) Who was that old woman?

CIUACOATL

Why, no one!

SÁNCHEZ

It's so cold. Have you any of that wonderful chocolate?

CIUACOATL

Xocoatl? Go around by the kitchen, the cook is churning up a pot.

SÁNCHEZ

So warm, so sweet, so foamy. Don't turn your back on me. What's wrong, Cecilia?

CIUACOATL

My name is Ciuacoatl.

SÁNCHEZ

Ci . . . ua . . . coatl. Very difficult to pronounce. Cecilia is much sweeter—like your chocolate.

CIUACOATL

I better go, I hear my mistress stirring.

SÁNCHEZ

How is she?

CIUACOATL

Does a huracán spend itself in one night? Its wind and rain beat the land for days on end. What do you care? It was your master made her this way.

SÁNCHEZ

Still, he cares for her. He puts me here to guard her gate from dusk to dawn.

CIUACOATL

To spy on her.

SÁNCHEZ

To protect her.

CIUACOATL

She has no fear of anyone.

SÁNCHEZ

She has made many enemies.

CIUACOATL

And this is how she is repaid. Where is your valiant captain now?

SÁNCHEZ

At the cathedral preparing for his wedding with Doña Catalina.

CIUACOATL

Doña Catalina. Is it true she is white as a swan?

SÁNCHEZ

As white as the snow atop Popocatepetl. (*Mispronouncing it badly.*)

CIUACOATL

(*Pronouncing it correctly.*) Popocatepetl. Anyone that white must be ugly.

SÁNCHEZ

Look at me, I'm white. I'm not that ugly, am I?

CIUACOATL

I don't know. I can't tell what color you are. Don't you ever bathe? We bathe every day.

SÁNCHEZ

I like you, you're sharp and saucy like your famous chilies.

CIUACOATL

(*A cry is heard from within the house.*) My mistress!

SÁNCHEZ

Cecilia—there's going to be a big feast after the wedding.

CIUACOATL

She comes this way! Go!

SÁNCHEZ

There will be plenty to eat.

CIUACOATL

Go away, I say! (*SÁNCHEZ exits. Enter LA MALINCHE.*)

MALINCHE

Bring me my son! Where is my son?

CIUACOATL

In his room, asleep.

MALINCHE

I had a nightmare. I dreamed my son was in chain mail mounted on a beast with a sword in one hand and a cross in the other. He looked like a Spaniard! (*Beat.*) Hide him from his father.

CIUACOATL

Yes, Malintzin!

MALINCHE

My son! You are better off dead!

CIUACOATL

Don't say that.

MALINCHE

There is no future for him here.

CIUACOATL

But his father is the most powerful man in all of Mexico.

MALINCHE

His father is the most hated man in all of Mexico. (*Beat.*) What father denies his son and forsakes his wife? A father who has been too busy cavorting with his Spanish whore to see us. He has only known her for seven days. And we were with him for seven years! Tezcatlipoca! (*Turning to leave.*)

CIUACOATL

Malintzin, where are you going?

MALINCHE

To the Zócalo, the cathedral, to talk to my husband!

CIUACOATL

Why, why go there? Don't give your enemies cause to scorn or humiliate you.

MALINCHE

Their words don't bother me. But I will face him who betrayed me! (*Exit MALINCHE and CIUACOATL.*)

SÁNCHEZ

(*Entering with CORTÉS.*) The bishop is here to see you. He's very impatient.

CORTÉS

Let him cool his heels. Any unusual movements in the city?

SÁNCHEZ

This morning, as I made my rounds, I saw that old woman again, crying and carrying an empty cradle.

CORTÉS

Could that be the one they call La Llorona? What about La Malinche?

SÁNCHEZ

She screamed all night, broke clay pots, cursed you, the bishop, God in heaven. Threatened to kill herself, you, the child.

CORTÉS

Keep her away from me, I don't want to see her.

SÁNCHEZ

Yes, my captain.

CORTÉS

Watch her carefully and bring me my son.

SÁNCHEZ

I'll have to do it by guile, for if she sees me taking him away she'll scratch my eyes out.

CORTÉS

There's a lot of storm and fury right now, but it soon will pass.

SÁNCHEZ

Women have long memories.

CORTÉS

I've hit upon a plan to appease her. These people hate to lose face.

SÁNCHEZ

She is angry you made no provisions for her or her son.

CORTÉS

Oh, but I have! (*The BISHOP abruptly enters the room.*) Sánchez, why did you keep the bishop waiting?

SÁNCHEZ

(*Bowing deeply.*) Pardon me. I meant no offense.

CORTÉS

You can make up for your insolence by bringing Bishop Lizárraga a glass of sherry.

BISHOP

No, no, I never drink this early in the day.

CORTÉS

Oh, but it's exquisite sherry, from Jerez de la Frontera.

BISHOP

¡Jerez de la Frontera! Well, in that case. (*SÁNCHEZ exits to get the sherry.*) Any word about the new viceroy?

CORTÉS

The last report is he landed in Vera Cruz. He should be here within twelve days.

BISHOP

That means we don't have very much time, do we?

CORTÉS

Well, my marriage to Catalina is a step in the right direction.

BISHOP

I must tell you, my niece is greatly displeased.

CORTÉS

Oh, why?

BISHOP

It's humiliating, having that woman in the same city as your wife-to-be. Why haven't you gotten rid of her?

CORTÉS

It's rather delicate, you see. The Indians, especially the common people, idolize her. Why, she's almost like a type of goddess.

BISHOP

A goddess, how irreverent! I don't understand, I thought the Aztec nobles hated her because she helped topple their empire. Look here, you can't be husband to two women. What kind of an example is that? It seems as if I were condoning it.

CORTÉS

You're so sanctimonious.

BISHOP

The church must be above reproach! I will not allow you to make a mockery of the holy sacrament of marriage. You know the viceroy will use anything he can against you.

CORTÉS

Very well, I'll get rid of her. (*SÁNCHEZ enters and serves the sherry. He stays discreetly out of the way, yet listens in on the conversation.*)

BISHOP

Ah, the sherry! And so, I have your word. (*They drink.*) Excellent! One more thing, the child goes with his mother.

CORTÉS

My son? No. Martín is my first-born son, my flesh and blood.

BISHOP

But you'll have other children with my niece.

SÁNCHEZ

But Martín is the spitting image of his father.

BISHOP

(*To SÁNCHEZ, in jest.*) Albeit several shades darker!

CORTÉS

This is a cub who will grow into a lion. The way he rides a horse, as though born to the saddle. Martín will be the bulwark of my old age, the second in a long line of conquistadores.

BISHOP

Vanity. You wish to populate the New World with your progeny.

CORTÉS

(*Trying to pour the BISHOP some more sherry.*) More sherry?

BISHOP

No, I have to say Mass. (*He gets up to leave, then stops before reaching the door.*) I want to set things right before the arrival of the viceroy. You won't disappoint us, will you?

CORTÉS

Of course not. (*Exit the BISHOP.*) Cursed old fool!

SÁNCHEZ

   Now, what are you going to do about La Malinche?

CORTÉS

   She's become too demanding, too possessive. I'm not the kind of man
   who gives himself over to a woman.

SÁNCHEZ

   But your son stays with you.

CORTÉS

   Yes, I'll persuade her it's the best thing for everyone.

SÁNCHEZ

   You'll have to move a mountain to do that. She'll fight like a tiger to
   keep her cub.

CORTÉS

   I know. She's liable to do anything. Go and fetch Martín. I'll inform
   her after the fact.

SÁNCHEZ

   Yes, my captain. (*Exit SÁNCHEZ and CORTÉS.*)

BISHOP

   (*Entering with LA MALINCHE at the gates to the cathedral.*) You
   have no business here. I see malice in your eyes.

MALINCHE

   Who bred it there?

BISHOP

   I care not. Accept it, your union is dissolved. Hernán Cortés, captain
   general of New Spain, is to be wed to my niece, Catalina.

MALINCHE

   But he and I have lived as man and woman for seven years.

BISHOP

   Not in the eyes of the church.

MALINCHE

   In the eyes of heaven and earth we were one! We have a son.

BISHOP

   A bastard, half-breed!

MALINCHE

Your words cut into my flesh.

BISHOP

Marina, I advise you to leave. Otherwise, it will go very badly for you. There are those who want to see you punished.

MALINCHE

Who? Why? After all I did for Cortés and the Crown?

BISHOP

I've heard the story, how you were sold into slavery by your own people, given to Cortés as tribute, quickly learned Castellano, and became his principal translator.

MALINCHE

He spoke though my lips.

BISHOP

Did the Indians actually think you were giving the orders?

MALINCHE

I was the medium by which he communicated. I put myself in the middle of the conflict and intervened in the plot. I was his adviser, secretary, and messenger.

BISHOP

You give yourself more importance than is due.

MALINCHE

I became part of him. My people could not conceive of Cortés without me. They called him "Hue-Hue Malintzin, the old captain who brings Doña Marina."

BISHOP

Like the way they conceived of the horse and rider as one? The Indian concept of duality?

MALINCHE

A unique being was created through our union. He spoke through my mouth like a priest who transmits the word of God.

BISHOP

Don't be disrespectful!

MALINCHE

Tell me, who speaks of banishing me? Let my accusers show their faces.

BISHOP

You've made some powerful enemies, Marina. Certain Aztec nobles have told me stories of your black powers, your magic arts. They say you still practice those abominations despite professing Christianity.

MALINCHE

They libel me because I am a woman who helped topple their oppressive pyramids. They used the common people as sacrificial slaves.

BISHOP

Is it true, at night, people tell stories of you to their children to frighten them?

MALINCHE

You are confusing me with Ciuapipiltzin.

BISHOP

Ci-ua-pipil-tzin?

MALINCHE

La Llorona. An Aztec goddess who carries an empty cradle, looking and lamenting for her lost children.

BISHOP

How did she lose her children, this "goddess"?

MALINCHE

She drowned them in the lake and thus is doomed to wander for all eternity.

BISHOP

Why did she kill her children? What a repulsive thing! Who is she? Where does she reside?

MALINCHE

Why, she's here, there!

BISHOP

(*Frightened.*) Where?

MALINCHE

Everywhere!

BISHOP

Well then, we must stamp out this idolatry! Tell me where she is!

MALINCHE

Bishop Lizárraga, I'm afraid that's impossible.

BISHOP

  Why, what do you mean?

MALINCHE

  In order to see La Llorona, one has to believe in her! (*Blackout.*)

LLORONA

  (*Entering with a broken spear in her hand.*)
    Broken spears lie in the road
    We ripped the hair from our scalps
    Our houses are roofless now, the walls red with blood
    Worms swarm in the streets and plazas, where bodies lay bloated
    The water has turned red
    When we drink it, it has the taste of brine
    We have pounded our heads in despair against the adobe walls
    Our inheritance, our city, is lost
    The shields of our warriors were its defense
    Now they lie useless on the ground
    We have chewed dry twigs and salt grasses
    We have filled our mouths with dust and bits of adobe
    We have eaten lizards, rats, and worms
    But still we are hungry. (*LA LLORONA exits.*)

CORTÉS

  (*In front of MALINCHE's house, pounding on her door.*) Open up!
  Open up in there! Where is my son?

MALINCHE

  (*Appearing at the door.*) I knew that would get you to come.

CORTÉS

  Why are you hiding him?

MALINCHE

  Why are you marrying another woman? Why didn't you tell me
  about this marriage?

CORTÉS

  My thoughts belong to me, I share them with no one!

MALINCHE

  But haven't you always confided in me? Who warned you at Cholula
  that the enemy was planning a surprise night attack?

CORTÉS

  You.

MALINCHE

And didn't you confess your forebodings to me that sad night, La Noche Triste, when hundreds of your comrades drowned in the canals, laden down by their gold and avarice?

CORTÉS

Yes.

MALINCHE

Then, why can't you face me? I who was your comrade in arms. I who nursed you back to health when you were sick!

CORTÉS

Marina, I do not disdain your services as translator, counselor, cook, and nurse. But the Conquest was much more than that. It was the horses that shocked, the gunpowder that spat lead, the swords forged in Toledo.

MALINCHE

It was the plague you carried in your bodies that wiped us out!

CORTÉS

Call it Divine Intervention, just like the signs that presaged my coming that had Moctezuma cowed before I even set foot in Mexico. Was it not the Holy Cross and our Blessed Virgin of Guadalupe whom I carried from my land of Extremadura and set in every town and village?

MALINCHE

Yes, but who gained the confidence of the Native people, who paved your way?

CORTÉS

Sooner or later, I would have battered down the walls.

MALINCHE

At a tremendous cost of Spanish lives!

CORTÉS

Very well, I owe you an enormous debt. Are you satisfied?

MALINCHE

I put the riches of Mexico at your feet! I bore your son!

CORTÉS

He is the best prize of all!

MALINCHE

Don't you understand? We are the family of this new nation. How can you throw that away? Hernán, it's not too late for you to change your mind!

CORTÉS

Forget about it, Marina, forget about us.

MALINCHE

How can I forget you who took me from my native village, who taught me the Spanish tongue, and from whose lips I also learned another language, love?

CORTÉS

Don't speak of love to me, I don't know what it is.

MALINCHE

Call off the wedding!

CORTÉS

I have given my word of honor.

MALINCHE

Words are empty, follow your destiny. We are a union you cannot dissolve!

CORTÉS

You know I'm not marrying for love.

MALINCHE

What, then? What can that pale, sickly thing give you?

CORTÉS

I have made a great many enemies.

MALINCHE

Haven't we always fought them off together?

CORTÉS

Jackals do not stand and fight. They hide in the king's court. A lion brought home the prize, and the milk-fed Hidalgos want to share in the spoils! Marina, I am the son of a good Christian family, but I am not of noble blood.

MALINCHE

I see. This has something to do with the new viceroy.

CORTÉS

By marrying Bishop Lizárraga's niece, who is related to the Crown by blood, I strengthen my position, both at home and in the court.

MALINCHE

But I am your wife, your partner, your queen!

CORTÉS

But you are also a . . .

MALINCHE

What? Go on, say it. Coward! I am Aztec, what you call an Indian! Not worthy to marry a noble white man like you!

CORTÉS

Marina, you knew that . . .

MALINCHE

What happened to all those fine words about the "new race of man," the "mestizo," who would populate this New World? Didn't you point to our son as an example of this new breed?

CORTÉS

Don't think I haven't made provisions for you. And him, especially him. I intend to petition Pope Clemente VII to make Martín legitimate!

MALINCHE

Legitimate? The pope can make Martín legitimate? How, why, for what reason?

CORTÉS

How? By issuing a special dispensation—and believe me, it'll cost me a pretty penny! Why? So our son will gain respectability.

MALINCHE

Respectability!

CORTÉS

If Martín achieves legitimacy, he will be accepted into society and marry into a noble family!

MALINCHE

I see . . . your intentions are "noble."

CORTÉS

And as for you, Marina, what do you say to a fine home in Orizaba with a generous landholding and peons to till it?

MALINCHE

In Orizaba? Oh, I see it all now! You'll have two houses, a big house here in Mexico and a small one in Orizaba. (*CORTÉS shakes his head "no."*) She will be your lawful wedded wife, and I will be your . . . concubine!

CORTÉS

Marina, Juan Jaramillo has consented to marry you.

MALINCHE

Juan Jaramillo!

CORTÉS

That is how I will provide for you. By marrying you off to a Spanish gentleman! In the eyes of the law, you will be legitimate—just like Martín!

MALINCHE

Legitimate? Legitimate!

CORTÉS

It's the only way, Marina, the only way!

MALINCHE

Tezcatlipoca! Tezcatlipoca! (*MALINCHE throws herself on CORTÉS, beating on him with her fists. He restrains her by wrapping his arms around her. Enter LA LLORONA as flutes and drums play. She causes a transformation to occur and watches as the couple embrace, lie down together, and fall asleep.*)

LLORONA

(*Stage whisper.*) Malintzin! Malintzin! Get up!

MALINCHE

Who is it?

LLORONA

Wake up!

MALINCHE

Where am I?

LLORONA

Cholula. Don't wake him. Tonight the Cholutecas attack the whites.

MALINCHE

What! I must warn him!

LLORONA

No. It's time for him to die. Why must the white man always win?

MALINCHE

Because his fate is tied with mine.

LLORONA

Are you becoming one of them? (*MALINCHE does not answer.*) My child, do not delude yourself, they will never accept you!

MALINCHE

I know who I am, and I belong with him!

LLORONA

The Spaniard?

MALINCHE

The man.

LLORONA

He's using you. Your knowledge of tribes, customs, and languages. Without you, he is lost, or dead.

MALINCHE

Let him feel indebted to me.

LLORONA

He will betray you! Your own people will grow to despise you. Malintzin, what is happening to you?

MALINCHE

In my womb a child is growing who has his blood and mine. And this child I cannot betray!

LLORONA

I see! It's too late, the deed is done
They came in the year Ce Acatl, 1519
The first of nine fifty-two-year hell cycles
And toppled our temples
We fell like rubble and lay scattered
On the face of the earth

But, like a volcano that lies dormant
One day we shall erupt. (*Exit LA LLORONA.*)

*Crossover. Images of life after the Conquest, like a dumb show. LA MALINCHE and CORTÉS standing on a rooftop, CORTÉS giving orders, LA MALINCHE translating for the Natives below. Afterward, both alight from the roof and are joined by MARTÍN. We see a domestic scene, as though in a Diego Rivera mural: the white CORTÉS, the Aztec MALINCHE, the mestizo MARTÍN. They exit.*

*The next scene is the cathedral where the BISHOP encounters what appears to be a young Indian woman sitting on the steps of the church. He stares at her.*

WOMAN

Are you looking for someone, my lord?

BISHOP

Not especially. (*Beat.*) Who are you?

WOMAN

I am no one, my lord.

BISHOP

No need to sit out here, good woman. Come inside the church to pray.

WOMAN

Are you looking for me, my lord?

BISHOP

Why no. Should I be?

WOMAN

Would one such as I be welcome in your church, my lord?

BISHOP

This is your house, good woman. As long as you do not pray to false gods.

WOMAN

I pray to the God of the Close Vicinity, to whom the heavens and earth belong.

BISHOP

You mean Jesus Christ?

WOMAN

I mean our Lord and Lady Ometecuhtli—Omecihuatl, mother and father. They are the mirror of day and night, the star that illuminates, the shining skirt of stars, in Tonan, in Tota.

BISHOP

You are confusing the Blessed Mother with God the Father.

WOMAN

Did not the mother and father make the son?

BISHOP

Yes, of course . . .

WOMAN

Well then . . .

BISHOP

Young woman, do not sit there in darkness. Come into the bosom of the church so that we may enlighten you.

WOMAN

My lord, my very esteemed lord, great hardships have we endured since you came to our country. We ignorant people have heard you, but you have not listened in return.

BISHOP

Come, you must pray to the true God.

WOMAN

My lord! You say we do not know the true God! Painful words are those you speak; because of them I am disturbed, I am troubled.

BISHOP

We will turn your confusion into clarity.

WOMAN

Our ancestors are unaccustomed to speaking thus; they who taught us how to worship, bleed ourselves in penitence, burn incense, sacrifice.

BISHOP

No! No more sacrifices. No more blood sprayed on the altars. No more men flayed of their skin.

WOMAN

Your God was sacrificed.

BISHOP

That was different!

WOMAN

I have seen him nailed and bleeding on his cross. So it was with our Gods. We live because of their sacrifice.

BISHOP

Who are you? You are a very clever woman.

WOMAN

I am no one special, my lord.

BISHOP

Enough of this. Come, I will teach you the catechism.

WOMAN

My lord, I am not worthy.

BISHOP

I command you!

WOMAN

If my lord wishes.

BISHOP

I have been looking for someone like you.

WOMAN

Then, you have found me!

BISHOP

You are still young. There is time for you to learn.

WOMAN

Learn what, my lord?

BISHOP

Many things. Remove your shawl, let me look upon your face. (*As she removes her shawl.*) You're very pretty.

WOMAN

Pretty! Oh, you flatter me, my lord. (*As he holds on to her.*) What do you see?

BISHOP

The face of an angel!

WOMAN

What do you feel?

BISHOP

Rapture! After you are baptized, you shall become my personal servant.

WOMAN

(*Breaking away from him.*) And your whore!

BISHOP

(*This stops him cold.*) My desires are not carnal. (*She hides behind an alcove.*)

WOMAN (*Voice*)

Neither am I of the flesh.

BISHOP

(*Going after her.*) What are you then?

WOMAN

(*LA LLORONA appears as a skeleton with red eyes and sharpened teeth.*) This is the real me!

BISHOP

(*Screaming, beside himself.*) Witch! Witch! Enchantress! Guards! Guards! (*LA LLORONA disappears.*)

SÁNCHEZ

(*Entering.*) Are you all right?

BISHOP

(*Visibly shaken.*) Did you see her? Did you see that?

SÁNCHEZ

The woman? Yes, I caught a glimpse of her.

BISHOP

Who is she? Have you seen her before?

SÁNCHEZ

I saw her this morning. In front of Doña Marina's house.

BISHOP

Post extra guards at the gates. Let no one enter tomorrow who is not a member of the wedding party.

SÁNCHEZ

Yes, my lord.

BISHOP

Come with me to La Malinche's house. (*They exit.*)

MALINCHE

(*Entering with CORTÉS as before.*) You try to appease me by giving me to one of your drunken soldiers!

CORTÉS

I offer you payment for your services!

MALINCHE

I am not a whore you can buy.

CORTÉS

I shall not make this offer twice.

MALINCHE

You are but a shell of the man I once knew.

CORTÉS

Say what you want, do what you will. But I am to be married to Catalina tomorrow.

MALINCHE

Catalina! The young Spanish goose has a name.

CORTÉS

Enough of your insults!

MALINCHE

Weakling! Coward! I made you who you are! Without me, you are nothing!

CORTÉS

Get out of my sight! (*Raising his hand to strike her!*)

MALINCHE

You conquer women now, not warriors.

CORTÉS

Serpent-tongued slattern! That's not all! I'm taking my son away from you!

MALINCHE

Ah, what! That too! (*Beat.*) Hernán, you don't need Martín. Your Spanish bitch will whelp you a white litter!

CORTÉS

You are not a fit mother to raise him. (*Grabbing her hair and twisting it.*) Now, tell me where he is or I'll pull your hair out!

MALINCHE

You'll never find him. I've hidden him from you forever.

CORTÉS

You ignorant Indian! I civilized you!

MALINCHE

And Moctezuma thought you were a god!

CORTÉS

(*Throwing her on the floor.*) I am glad to be rid of you, Malinche. You are like a serpent choking me.

MALINCHE

And you are a dagger at my heart.

CORTÉS

If you don't turn over my son I will slay you and your entire household. Sánchez! Sánchez!

SÁNCHEZ

(*Entering.*) Yes, my captain.

CORTÉS

Go inside the house and bring Malinche's servant, Cecilia.

SÁNCHEZ

Cecilia, sir?

CORTÉS

Yes, I'll bet she knows where Martín is. (*To MALINCHE.*) Do you think she'll survive the torture . . . like your Aztec prince Cuauhtemoc. (*To SÁNCHEZ.*) Just don't stand there like a statue, go!

SÁNCHEZ

Yes sir!

MALINCHE

You have made a great enemy of one who was your loyal friend.

CORTÉS

But at last I am rid of your spell! I can breathe free!

MALINCHE

You will never be rid of me. I will always be inside you, the only woman who really knows you. More than your own mother! Look at me. Look at my face! You will never gaze upon another woman without seeing me!

CORTÉS

(*He turns away from her in disgust. Enter SÁNCHEZ, obviously under great stress, bringing in CIUACOATL.*) Don't let either one of them out of your sight. (*Enter the BISHOP. CORTÉS goes to him. They conspire in whispers.*)

SÁNCHEZ

(*To CIUACOATL.*) Tell him where the child is!

BISHOP

(*To CORTÉS, as he points to LA MALINCHE.*) There's something evil in our midst, and she is the cause of it.

CORTÉS

Where is my son? (*Beat.*) Sánchez! Draw your sword! (*The BISHOP turns his back as SÁNCHEZ draws his short sword.*) Hold it at Cecilia's throat! (*SÁNCHEZ hesitates.*) Do it! (*SÁNCHEZ does so.*) Now, will someone tell me? No? (*Going first to CIUACOATL, then MALINCHE.*) No? Sánchez! Cut her throat! Now! (*SÁNCHEZ is beside himself, not knowing whom to obey, his master or his heart.*)

MALINCHE

No! Wait! Ciuacoatl—take them to Martín.

CORTÉS

(*Aside to SÁNCHEZ.*) I'll get my son, you guard the bishop. (*Exit CIUACOATL, followed by CORTÉS.*)

BISHOP

(*Approaching MALINCHE.*) As for you, I warned you not to cause trouble.

MALINCHE

I did nothing wrong!

BISHOP

Marina-Malinche, I hereby banish you forever from this city. Leave today, at once, I have spoken.

MALINCHE

I can't possibly leave at such short notice.

BISHOP

I don't care. Pack what you can carry and leave the city. I'm only doing this as a favor for Cortés. You should be burned at the stake!

MALINCHE

But I've done nothing wrong! Just give me one more day to sort out my affairs.

BISHOP

I don't want you here the day of the wedding.

MALINCHE

But sir, what do you, a powerful and learned man, have to fear from a poor Indian woman like myself?

BISHOP

You threatened me and my niece. You have performed acts of black magic.

MALINCHE

Lies, sir, lies. Please, it's so late in the day. All I am asking for is time to collect my belongings and put my affairs in order.

BISHOP

What you say seems innocent enough. Yet in my heart I feel you are plotting some evil. You are too clever. You know when to hold your tongue and when to speak.

MALINCHE

(*Getting down on her knees and touching the hem of his robe.*) I beg of you, sir, please, have pity!

BISHOP

(*Pulling away.*) Don't touch me!

MALINCHE

I pray you!

BISHOP

Your pagan prayers?

MALINCHE

I'm a Christian.

BISHOP

When it's to your advantage.

MALINCHE

Please, your Holiness, just one more day. In the name of the Virgin
Mary!

BISHOP

Don't use her name in vain.

MALINCHE

Sir, I have a confession to make. I know where the cult of
Ciuapipiltzin is located!

BISHOP

La Llorona!

MALINCHE

Yes, and in order to prove I am a Christian, I am willing to tell you
where you may find her!

BISHOP

I knew it! I saw her! Is she a skeleton with red eyes and sharpened
teeth like knives?

MALINCHE

Yes, that is but one of her manifestations! (*The BISHOP crosses
himself.*) Ciuapipiltzin lives, the people still worship her.

BISHOP

Where?

MALINCHE

Her temple lies in a secret catacomb near the cathedral!

BISHOP

Near the cathedral! (*To MALINCHE.*) If this is true, I'll grant your
request to stay an extra day. But if I see you anywhere near the
wedding party, I'll have you hanged! (*Exit SÁNCHEZ and BISHOP.*)

LLORONA

(*Entering, speaking to the audience.*)
    The bad potter is careless
    He ignores the look of things
    He is greedy, he scorns other people
    Like a vulture with a shrouded heart
    Sluggish, coarse, weak

The things he makes are inferior
He ruins everything that he touches
The good potter takes great pains with his work
He molds the clay into likeness
He converses with his heart
He makes things alike, creates them
He knows all, as though he were a Toltec.

MALINCHE

(*To LA LLORONA.*) You heard what I told the bishop?

LLORONA

I'll be there, waiting for him.

MALINCHE

Ciuapipiltzin, they are going to take away my son! Is there time to save him and flee far away from here?

LLORONA

Where would you go? Who would receive you? He is neither Aztec nor Spanish. The men of our race would kill him. And the whites look down on him because of his Native blood.

MALINCHE

Either way he is damned. Then there is no hope for us? (*LA LLORONA does not answer.*) What a fool I was to imagine myself a Spanish Doña.

LLORONA

You are an Aztec priestess.

MALINCHE

I want to return to what I am.

LLORONA

Renew your faith! Where is your obsidian mirror?

MALINCHE

That reflection of my Mechica soul . . .

LLORONA

(*Handing her a mirror.*) Here it is, the image of the black Tezcat-lipoca. Gaze into it and draw your strength.

MALINCHE

Tezcatlipoca! I lost sight of you when I served the white man. Now I return to you, Smoking Mirror!

LLORONA

Drink, drink the reflection. Dive into its profound reaches—queen, magician, sorceress! What is your wish?

MALINCHE

Death! Death to them all!

LLORONA

What form?

MALINCHE

Go the way in which we are most skillful.

BOTH

Poison!

MALINCHE

Prepare me the most powerful poison conceivable—enough to kill a thousand Spaniards. (*As LA LLORONA prepares it.*) Bitter I will make their marriage bed, bitter the wedding and the casting me out of the city, bitter the taking of my child. So, bishop, wife, and husband, you must die!

LLORONA

Here is the potion. It has the bile of the deadly blowfish, the venom of the rattlesnake, the sting of the scorpion. It will stick like tar to anything, yet leave no trace or odor. Should a moist hand touch it, the flesh would be set afire.

MALINCHE

Thank you, Ciuapipiltzin! Thank you, Teztcatlipoca! (*LA LLORONA bows and exits.*)

CORTÉS

(*At the cathedral, watching SÁNCHEZ excavate what appears to be a tomb.*) What does the bishop hope to find?

SÁNCHEZ

I don't know, but his men were digging here.

CORTÉS

(*Joking.*) Let me know if you find Moctezuma's gold! Damn him, always snooping around. (*Noticing the BISHOP approaching.*) Shhh, here he comes!

BISHOP

(*Approaching with a torch.*) Any discoveries?

CORTÉS

Not much, only a few shards of pottery.

BISHOP

Did you know this was the site of the Templo Mayor?

CORTÉS

Of course, I tore it down! We used the same bricks to build the cathedral.

BISHOP

That was a mistake, an abomination!

CORTÉS

Come now, do you really think a cult like this could flourish right under our very noses?

BISHOP

Oh yes, these people are deceitful. They feign conversion to the Catholic faith and laugh at us behind their Aztec faces. What news of the viceroy?

CORTÉS

He should be here within a fortnight. But then, you already know that, don't you?

BISHOP

What are you insinuating?

CORTÉS

That you're meeting with the viceroy's men and plotting against me.

BISHOP

Spying on me, now?

CORTÉS

I have every right to be. I conquered these lands and gave their riches to the king of Spain. But what do I get in return?

SÁNCHEZ

(*Pulling aside a stone.*) I think I found something!

CORTÉS

Look! A stone idol! (*SÁNCHEZ exposes what looks like the figure of Coyolxauhqui.*)

SÁNCHEZ

It's a stone disk . . . of a woman . . . with her head cut off!

CORTÉS

Her body ripped to pieces.

BISHOP

To think that this abomination lay underneath our holy cathedral.

SÁNCHEZ

It doesn't surprise me, my grace. After all, we Spaniards are but a pool in a sea of Aztecs.

BISHOP

What does that have to do with anything, you simpleton!

SÁNCHEZ

Beg your pardon, my grace, but sometimes I wonder whether we really conquered them, or they just swallowed us up.

CORTÉS

Sánchez . . .

SÁNCHEZ

You see, underneath the foundations of our church lies the real Mexico!

BISHOP

Brilliant deduction, brilliant!

CORTÉS

Wait, there's something here. We've been thinking of a way to convert the Indians. I mean, really convert them. Not this superficial sprinkling of Holy Water.

BISHOP

Don't be sacrilegious, man!

CORTÉS

But what if the Virgin de Guadalupe, who I brought from my home-land of Extremadura and put in every heathen temple, were to miraculously appear in Tenochtitlan?

BISHOP

The Virgin appear here! How?

CORTÉS

By a miracle of grace.

BISHOP

I don't understand. What are you suggesting?

CORTÉS

A sleight of hand, an artful staging . . .

BISHOP

The reports are true. You are mad!

CORTÉS

What's the difference between that and baptizing ten thousand Indians at one time? In due time they will learn the True Faith.

BISHOP

I see your point, but perpetuating a fraud of that magnitude . . .

CORTÉS

Think of it, the Virgin appears in Tepeyac, where they worship the cult of Tonanztin, the eater of filth.

BISHOP

I find it repugnant!

CORTÉS

You don't understand, she's "the eater of sins." They confess their sins to her, just as we confess our sins to Guadalupe.

BISHOP

My God, man, have you no shame?

CORTÉS

But you shall see how the end justifies the means!

BISHOP

(*Laughing with CORTÉS, despite himself.*) This is the very height of cynicism! (*Blackout.*)

*The front of LA MALINCHE's house. Enter CIUACOATL and MALINCHE.*

CIUACOATL

I am going to gather our things.

MALINCHE

Wait, there are more important matters.

CIUACOATL

Like what?

MALINCHE

A wedding offering for the bride and groom.

CIUACOATL

What are you thinking of?

MALINCHE

Revenge! I prostrated myself before the bishop to gain some precious time. Go to the house and take out my mother's gold headdress with its brilliant quetzal feathers. Also her huipil of finely woven gold thread.

CIUACOATL

But that is your inheritance.

MALINCHE

Exactly. The Spanish avarice for gold will be bait for my trap.

CIUACOATL

Your rage will consume us all.

MALINCHE

I will tell Cortés the match with his Spanish bride was a sound idea. But it will only be a ruse to get them to accept the gifts. You see, all who touch them will die.

CIUACOATL

Malintzin, my little flower, my precious quetzal. I watched you grow from a doe, unsteady on thin legs, into a swift and graceful deer. Together we learned about herbs and roots, our puberty rites. I watched you dance, sleek and dark, a panther in the moonlight. Forget Hernán Cortés, forget this self-destructive desire for revenge.

MALINCHE

It was everything to think well of one man, but the only man I ever loved turned out to be a liar.

CIUACOATL

Not all men are liars, Malintzin.

MALINCHE

Oh, my father! Why did you give me to the bearded ones? Oh, my country! Why did I speak for the Spaniards?

CIUACOATL

Malintzin, do not blame yourself. You were given to the white man in return for the safety of our village. They would have burned it and killed everyone. We are slaves; first to our fathers, then to our husbands.

MALINCHE

And marriage is the worst form of slavery. Go—bring Cortés to me. The time of their demise is near.

CIUACOATL

Malintzin, please, it is too dangerous.

MALINCHE

We have to. Don't you see—he'll take Martín away and raise him as a Spaniard. He'll turn him against our people and use him just as he used me!

CIUACOATL

But suppose the husband, bride, and bishop dead . . .

MALINCHE

No, wait! (*Beat.*) I have a worse fate for my husband—let him live!

CIUACOATL

How will we escape the city? All the bridges leading out are well guarded.

MALINCHE

There is no escape! We must all die!

CIUACOATL

All die! Even your son? Has the milk in your breasts turned sour? You are ill-prepared, I want no part of this.

MALINCHE

Then go! Leave my sight! Traitor! And never return.

CIUACOATL

Malintzin . . .

MALINCHE

Ciuacoatl. In the name of Tezcatlipoca, will you join me in this pact?

CIUACOATL

I am not afraid of dying. But promise we will save Martín. He must live! He will fight for us! He will be our champion! A fisherman told me of a secret canal overgrown by reeds where we can flee the city.

MALINCHE

Is it possible? Can we all escape?

CIUACOATL

We must try!

MALINCHE

Very well. Pay him whatever price he asks. Take this poison. Be very careful! Don't touch it. Sprinkle it over the presents. You attend the wedding to observe. Have them bring Martín here—to see his father and me together one last time. (*Exit CIUACOATL.*)

Oh, my son! We must leave. But where shall we go?
Is there any place for us in all of Mexico?
Shall we go to the Quiche-Maya, where there is still a resistance?
Or north, among the Chichimeca, to live with the barbarians?
Is there any place on earth where the Spaniards do not rule!

LLORONA

(*Entering.*)
Where shall we go?
Oh, where can we go?
Is our home in the place of the dead?
In the interior of the heavens?
Or only here on earth
Is the abode of the dead?

(*LA LLORONA induces another vision in LA MALINCHE's mind. Enter CORTÉS, ragged and bleeding, barely able to carry his sword. He collapses next to a tree. It is the night of La Noche Triste.*)

MALINCHE

Do you remember La Noche Triste, that sad night
When hundreds of your comrades drowned in the canals
Laden down by their gold and avarice?

(*Walking into the "space" inhabited by CORTÉS.*)

CORTÉS

Malinche, once we were thirteen hundred Spanish soldiers and ninety-six horses . . . (*Starting to weep.*)

MALINCHE

It is raining, as if the night were crying! Let us take shelter under this ahuehuete tree.

CORTÉS

Now we are but four hundred men and twelve horses!

MALINCHE

Let me hold you in my arms, like a child, and drink your tears away!

CORTÉS

All my horses, all my men!

MALINCHE

Shhhhh, naked, vulnerable child Cortés!

CORTÉS

I lost eight hundred men today. Men who left Spain to follow me, common men, valiant men. In search of fortune, they took it to their watery graves!

MALINCHE

Tonight we'll sleep together wrapped in this horse's blanket.

CORTÉS

Are we lost Malinche?

MALINCHE

No, tomorrow we'll live to fight again!

CORTÉS

I am so tired.

MALINCHE

Sleep, sleep, we'll stay and sleep this sad night away. (*Blackout. Exit MALINCHE and CORTÉS.*)

*LA MALINCHE's house the next morning. Enter SÁNCHEZ with CIUACOATL.*

SÁNCHEZ

Is something the matter? You seem upset this morning.

CIUACOATL

Nothing, nothing.

SÁNCHEZ

Are you going to the feast with me?

CIUACOATL

Do you really think I would go where they will be celebrating the wedding of my mistress's husband to another woman?

SÁNCHEZ

I didn't think of it that way.

CIUACOATL

No, of course not. Men never think about anything except satisfying their own desires. You enjoy dominating us, force us to serve you, impose your will, then dispose of us—just like Cortés did to La Malinche.

SÁNCHEZ

Forgive me, I thought inviting you to the fiesta would please you. There's going to be a great deal of food and wine.

CIUACOATL

Besides, the bishop has forbidden my mistress or anyone of her house to go near the wedding.

SÁNCHEZ

That's true.

CIUACOATL

Nonetheless, I will go!

SÁNCHEZ

You will? You never cease to amaze me.

CIUACOATL

But I mustn't be noticed. I need an appropriate disguise. My mistress has some Spanish dresses Cortés gave her. No one must recognize me. (*She sees CORTÉS approaching.*) Let's go, here comes your master to see Malintzin! (*Exit SÁNCHEZ and CIUACOATL.*)

CORTÉS

(*Enter CORTÉS and LA MALINCHE.*) What urgent business do you claim on my wedding day?

MALINCHE

Hernán Cortés, captain general of New Spain, I beg you to forgive me. I am wrong, your arguments are sound. Why make an enemy of you or the bishop?

CORTÉS

I can't believe I am hearing you speak this way.

MALINCHE

I see now that you really care for Martín.

CORTÉS

He is the future, not us.

MALINCHE

You are right. He must be brought up under your protection. The Indian way has come to an end. Spain is the standard.

CORTÉS

Have you really come to your senses?

MALINCHE

I see now that, in your own way, you really do care for us. You baptized me, elevated me from slave to secretary, shared my bed, recognized our son as your own. And now you want to give us . . . legitimacy.

CORTÉS

These were contracts you entered into willingly.

MALINCHE

I only wish you would have told me about the marriage, trusted me. I might have stood by you when you wed this new wife. I might have even joined in the wedding and attended to you.

CORTÉS

Is this your sarcasm seeping through?

MALINCHE

No, I'm only being realistic. I was given to you during a time of war. That makes for temporary unions between people. I shouldn't have expected more. I accept your conditions.

CORTÉS

You will go to Orizaba with Jaramillo?

MALINCHE

No, that I will not do. I don't need you or any other man! My only wish is for Martín's happiness. What provisions have you made for him?

CORTÉS

He will be integrated with the children of my new issue.

MALINCHE

Will he be raised as a Spaniard . . . in a grand palace with his half brothers and sisters?

CORTÉS

Of course! And one day he will be crowned the marquis of the Valley of Oaxaca like his father.

MALINCHE

This is what you plan for my son?

CORTÉS

Yes, I will sire a field of Cortéses as a safeguard against our enemies in my old age.

MALINCHE

Then look, here comes Martín to greet you! (*Enter MARTÍN, accompanied by CIUACOATL.*)

CORTÉS

My little eagle!

MALINCHE

Martín, embrace your father. We have made our peace.

CORTÉS

My son. Your father will always care for you. You will become one of the lions of Mexico and grow up with the ruling class, a stronger man than your father's adversaries. (*MALINCHE turns away.*) But Marina, why is your visage so dark and melancholy? Why is your face turned away from us? Are these not the words you want to hear?

MALINCHE

It's just that I might not see him again, and the thought saddens me.

CORTÉS

He will be well cared for.

MALINCHE

But tell him. How will you assure us that your new wife will accept him?

CORTÉS

Why shouldn't she? He's my son!

MALINCHE

She'll be jealous and mistreat him.

CORTÉS

You don't know Catalina. She's kindhearted and giving of herself.

MALINCHE

I have some gifts to gain her sympathy—a finely woven huipil and a quetzal headdress. Ciuacoatl! A hundred ways is your bride blessed; her Spanish blood and the conqueror of Mexico to share her bed.

CORTÉS

Marina, keep your gifts. Do you think that a Spanish lady would wear the vestments of an Indian? (*Enter CIUACOATL carrying a black box.*)

MALINCHE

Ciuacoatl, open the chest. (*As CIUACOATL displays the gifts.*) Ah, but you see, Hernán, they are made of solid gold. Gold so fine and malleable your fingers leave an impression on it. Surely, your Spanish dama will not disdain this gift?

CORTÉS

¡Ave María!

MALINCHE

Careful, hold the chest by the handles. Don't touch the bride's wedding presents! It is bad luck . . . an affront against our customs.

CORTÉS

Why, this is the wealth of Moctezuma! You never told me you had riches like these.

MALINCHE

They are my family heirlooms. But for Martín's sake, I would give up all the gold in Mexico.

CORTÉS

The thought strikes me. Why not let our son personally hand these offerings to Catalina?

MALINCHE

No . . . I was thinking you . . .

CORTÉS

Martín! (*As the boy goes to him.*) You will go with me to the wedding. Afterward, stand in the receiving line and hand my bride these presents. Tell her you want to stay with your father. (*The boy nods his head "yes."*)

MALINCHE

But what if she rejects him? (*Church bells start to ring.*)

CORTÉS

I will be there to see that she doesn't. The church bells! It's time to go!

MALINCHE

> (*Aside to MARTÍN.*) Martín! Let the bride and only the bride reach into the chest! You must not touch the gifts at all! Do you understand? (*The boy agrees.*)

CORTÉS

> Hurry, Martín, a man cannot be late to his own wedding!

MALINCHE

> (*Still aside to MARTÍN.*) You return with Ciuacoatl right away! (*Exit MARTÍN and CORTÉS.*)

CIUACOATL

> See what you've done now! Martín's life is in danger.

MALINCHE

> Follow them. Get my son out of the cathedral the moment the bride accepts the gifts.

CIUACOATL

> The canoe is packed, and the fisherman awaits my signal!

MALINCHE

> Go quickly!

CIUACOATL

> I will take Martín directly there, by the old bridge, where the wild fowls nest.

MALINCHE

> We'll be reunited then. (*Exit CIUACOATL.*) Oh Tezcatlipoca. I can feel the noose tightening around my neck!

LLORONA

> (*Entering.*) Our Lord
> Ever present, ever close
> Thinks as he pleases
> Does as he wishes
> Mocks us
> As she wishes
> Has us in the palm of her hand
> Rolls us about
> Like pebbles we spin and bounce
> Flings us every which way
> We are but a diversion
> She laughs at us.

*(With a wide sweep of her hand, LA LLORONA brings forth the wedding of CATALINA and CORTÉS. Enter CATALINA, CORTÉS, SÁNCHEZ, the BISHOP, and MARTÍN, as though in a wedding processional. CATALINA puts on her wedding veil. A mime show takes place behind a scrim.)*

LLORONA

Look! It is Catalina, primping and preparing for her wedding ceremony.

MALINCHE

Is that her? My rival, Catalina? She is so young . . . and white as the snow atop Popocatepetl. She dances for sheer joy!

LLORONA

She will dance to any tune we play.

MALINCHE

They are at the receiving line now. Ah, I knew it! She refuses to greet or even acknowledge Martín!

CORTÉS

*(To CATALINA.)* Don't be angry, take these gifts and acknowledge my son.

LLORONA

She opens what will be her coffin. Her eyes light up upon seeing the treasure.

MALINCHE

Martín! Leave now! *(MARTÍN starts to leave.)*

LLORONA

The reception is over. Cortés is toasting and celebrating. *(The BISHOP drinks, obviously very tipsy.)* Catalina opens her presents.

MALINCHE

Hurry, Martín! Run to the front gates, to safety. *(MARTÍN exits.)*

LLORONA

She is trying on the dress. Now she places the golden crown on her head. Oh, she looks as fine and stately as an Aztec queen!

MALINCHE

She promenades back and forth, primping. Then all at once her face turns ashen. Her mouth, wanting to scream, emits only silence. She staggers backward as though shot by an arrow. Her trembling legs, wanting to take flight, crumble under her.

LLORONA

She sits up, all the while staring into the mirror, the smoking mirror. She tries to run, but another arrow pierces her body. She collapses, and her legs kick like a wounded deer. (*CORTÉS runs to her but doesn't touch her. There is consternation among the men.*)

MALINCHE

Look! She sits up! All the while staring into the smoking mirror. A white froth, like pulque, foams from her mouth. Her eyes roll back. Her tongue sticks out like a snake that coils around her throat!

LLORONA

The mirror smokes and burns!

MALINCHE

Tez-cat—li-poo-caaaaaaa!

LLORONA

Has answered your prayers!

MALINCHE

There is more, look!

LLORONA

(*Focus on the BISHOP behind the scrim.*) The bishop goes to his niece. The quetzal headdress on her hair bursts into flame. The gold huipil disintegrates on the horrified woman's flesh. She tosses her head from side to side trying to extinguish the fire—but it only fans the flames!

BISHOP

My dearest child—what devil has possessed you?

LLORONA

The hysterical woman runs into his arms, calling out the name of the Virgin Mary! The bishop tries to tear himself away from her clutches, but she sticks to him like tar. They are immolated!

MALINCHE

Justice! Justice!

LLORONA

His priestly raiments turn to cinder. Their skin melts from their bones. They crumble, blackened skeletons! (*Exit SÁNCHEZ and CORTÉS.*) Now you have it.

MALINCHE

Do I? Oh God!

CIUACOATL

(*Entering.*) Malinche, we have been discovered, the fisherman is dead!

MALINCHE

And Martín?

CIUACOATL

Nowhere to be found!

MALINCHE

Oh no!

LLORONA

(*Stoic.*) There is no escape. We are surrounded.

MALINCHE

Our enemies must not find him. How could I cheat fate? Everything is pointing in one direction. But what is wrong with me? How weak am I! I see now what I must do! I won't let them take my son like they took my husband! No, he can't fall victim to my enemies. (*Exit MALINCHE and CIUACOATL.*)

SÁNCHEZ

(*Entering with CORTÉS.*) My captain, the cathedral is on fire, and there is fighting in the Zócalo. The Indians have taken advantage of this to riot.

CORTÉS

She planned this, she got the Indians to turn on us!

SÁNCHEZ

Worse yet, the new viceroy just entered the city. He orders you to appear before him at once!

CORTÉS

They'll use this as an excuse to take my title and lands away! Find Malinche. Find Martín. One or the other. But bring her to me alive. I want her for myself! As for my son, hide him. They'll kill him for what his mother did. (*Exit SÁNCHEZ. CORTÉS starts to go in another direction and encounters LA LLORONA, who has been standing there all the time.*) Oh, my God—who are you?

LLORONA

The mother of us all, Cortés.

CORTÉS
    What?

LLORONA
    I am she of the starry skirt, she whose radiance envelops; she who is
    clothed in black, she who is clothed in red; lady of our flesh, lord of
    our flesh.

CORTÉS
    You know where La Malinche is!

LLORONA
    Yes, I do!

CORTÉS
    Tell me, or I'll kill you! (*Drawing a short sword.*)

LLORONA
    You cannot kill me . . . I'm already dead!

CORTÉS
    Keep away from me! What do you want?

LLORONA
    (*Snatching his sword away.*) Only this! (*She mysteriously disappears.
    He runs away in the opposite direction.*)

SÁNCHEZ
    (*Entering with CIUACOATL and MARTÍN on another part of the
    stage.*) Where are you going with that child?

CIUACOATL
    Somewhere, anywhere. His life is in danger.

SÁNCHEZ
    But so is yours. Where is that devil—your mistress?

CIUACOATL
    Inside the house. Take her . . . if you can. But let us go.

SÁNCHEZ
    His only possible salvation is with his father. Give him to me.

CIUACOATL
    For what? So he can be raised a Spaniard—a liar, thief, plunderer? To
    be an instrument in the destruction of his own people?

SÁNCHEZ

Cecilia, I've never lied to you.

CIUACOATL

You're just like all the others.

SÁNCHEZ

They're going to kill you for helping La Malinche. I can hide you. Come!

CIUACOATL

No, we go our own way.

SÁNCHEZ

I can't let you take Cortés's child.

CIUACOATL

Martín is not his, he's ours! (*As she draws her dagger, SÁNCHEZ tries to disarm her. They struggle. She wounds him in the hand, but not before he takes the dagger away from her.*) Sánchez! You're bleeding! I'm sorry. (*MARTÍN runs into his mother's house.*)

SÁNCHEZ

(*MARTÍN, frightened, runs away.*) The child!

CIUACOATL

Martín, come back! We've got to get him away from his mother. God knows what she might do! (*They exit, following MARTÍN.*)

LLORONA

(*Entering.*) Truly do we live on earth
Not forever on earth: only a little while here
Although it be jade, it will be broken
Although it be gold, it is crushed
Although it be quetzal feather, it is torn asunder
Not forever on earth; only a little while here.

MALINCHE

(*Entering.*) Ciuapipiltzin! You who are doomed to wander for all eternity. I commit my soul unto your care! I too must join you. I too weep for what I must do! (*MARTÍN enters from the other side of the stage.*) Oh, my son! I can't look at you now without wanting to tear from your face the traces of him whom I hate!

LLORONA

(*Walking backstage behind the scrim to a pyramid-shaped altar.*) Martín!

MALINCHE

(*As MARTÍN walks toward his mother.*) In vain did I rear you and suffer the pain of childbirth. Never will I see you grow into a strong warrior. Never will I see you wed or wait on your bride and make your marriage bed. Once I had hopes that you might look after me in my old age and see my spirit carried into the great beyond. Oh heavens, pity me, but give me strength to do what must be done!

LLORONA

It is time, Malintzin!

MALINCHE

My little ocelotl, my little jaguar. We must go far away from here, we are not loved. People want us harmed. I entrust you to that lady. (*Pointing to LA LLORONA.*)

LLORONA

(*As MARTÍN walks up to the pyramid-shaped altar.*)
    Oh, my son, you have known hardship, you have endured
        suffering
    In truth, the abode of us is not here on earth
    Only for a moment, for an instant, do we warm ourselves in
        the sun.

MALINCHE

(*To MARTÍN.*) You must not be afraid!
    And now the Lord of the Region of the Dead takes you
    You will journey to Mictlan
    The place of the un-fleshed
    Where the journey ends
    A house with no smoke-hole, a house with no vent
    Never again shall you return
    Never again shall you be of the living.

(*A spotlight shines on LA LLORONA's face, which is now turned into a skull mask.*)

MALINCHE

Be strong, Martín, do not waver. You are a warrior! (*The light starts to fade, but not before LA LLORONA raises aloft the shining blade she took from CORTÉS, holding it over MARTÍN. LA MALINCHE screams. Blackout.*)

CORTÉS

(*Entering.*) She screams! Has someone else gotten to her before me?
Oh, vengeance! (*Trying to break down the gates to her house.*) Open!
Open, I say! Is she there? Has she killed herself?

MALINCHE

(*As the gates slowly open.*) What shadow of a man comes beating on
my door? (*MALINCHE has taken LLORONA's place atop the altar,
elevated, beyond CORTÉS's reach.*)

CORTÉS

I have come for you, Malinche!

MALINCHE

You're not the avenger, a higher power is.

CORTÉS

Where is my son?

MALINCHE

Shhhhh! He is sleeping. I might let you look at him, although you'll
never hold him in your arms again. Night has fallen. Shouldn't you
be home with your Spanish bride warming the royal bed?

CORTÉS

You will die with drops of venom dripping from your mouth.

MALINCHE

Captain . . . Hernán Cortés . . . would you like to see your son? Well,
here he is! (*Lights reveal MARTÍN's bloody body on the steps of the
altar.*)

CORTÉS

You sow! (*Rushing at her, trying to scale the pyramid.*) You ate your
farrow!

MALINCHE

You began this, not I.

CORTÉS

(*Falling down the incline.*) Loathsome viper! To do violence against
your own child!

MALINCHE

Why didn't you care for him when he was alive?

CORTÉS

How can you look another human being in the face after this? Malinche! I judge you along with all mankind. You will be known forever as the woman who murdered her child and betrayed her country.

MALINCHE

And you will be known as the beast who raped our land!

CORTÉS

Malinche! A cursed name!

MALINCHE

Cortés! A cursed name!

CORTÉS

Malinche! Yours alone! There will never be another Malinche in all of Mexico. Mothers will never give their daughters this name.

MALINCHE

Hernán Cortés! There will never be a statue of you in all of Mexico! But they will name a mountain after me!

CORTÉS

You will be alone until the end of time, take that to your grave!

MALINCHE

I accept my fate! As for you, degenerate conquistador, you will die one day of syphilis.

CORTÉS

(*Throwing his sword at her.*) Indian bitch! (*Beat.*) But why my son?

MALINCHE

It was my supreme sacrifice.

CORTÉS

You inhuman thing. You feel no sorrow?

MALINCHE

My grief is mine. At least you cannot mock it.

CORTÉS

Oh, my son, your mother's heart was infected.

MALINCHE

With a disease she caught from your father.

CORTÉS

It wasn't I who slit his throat.

MALINCHE

It was your blade, forged in Spain.

CORTÉS

He died because you did not want him raised a Spaniard?

MALINCHE

He died because you would not allow him to be raised a Mechica.

CORTÉS

Give me his little body so that I may bury him in a Christian way.

MALINCHE

No, you used your religion to deceive us.

CORTÉS

Have mercy on his soul!

MALINCHE

We will cleanse him in the lake, where Tlaloc reigns.

CORTÉS

God in heaven, is there no justice?

MALINCHE

Not in Tenochtitlan, Mexico

(*Lights fade on CORTÉS and MALINCHE. Enter CIUACOATL and SÁNCHEZ holding hands. They kneel and pray before the body of MARTÍN. Enter LA LLORONA carrying her empty cradle as before.*)

LLORONA

Everyone calls me the dark one,
Llorona, a spirit no one can see,
but I'm like a coal in the fire,
Llorona, red and hot as can be.
Oh, my Llorona, Llorona,
Llorona of now and then,
yesterday I was a wonder, Llorona,
today I am steeped in sin.
They say I feel no pity, Llorona,
because no one sees me crying,
well, dead men never make a sound, Llorona,
and painful is their dying.

It seems to me that the flowers, Llorona.
on graves are steadily creeping,
and when the wind blows, Llorona,
it looks as if they're weeping.

## The End

# Dreaming on a Sunday in the Alameda

## Characters

DIEGO RIVERA: Mexican artist

FRIDA KAHLO: Diego's wife and an artist in her own right; also
MORENA and CARMEN

HERNÁN CORTÉS: Conqueror of Mexico; also FATHER,
GENTLEMAN, and DON PORFIS

LA MALINCHE: Cortés's mistress and translator; also LA YERBERA
and LA CATRINA

JOHNNY: Diego's assistant

SOR JUANA INÉS DE LA CRUZ: Mexican poet of the seventeenth
century; also CHI-CHI, BLONDIE, NURSE

MONK, also DON GUILLERMO and POLICÍA

# Design Notes

*Since this is a play about a visual artist, it would help to have slides projected of Kahlo's and Rivera's work, especially* Sueño de una tarde dominical en la Alameda Central. *The images "frame" the scenes and serve as a point of reference. Sound cues are also essential in the heightening of this spectacle. Because there are so many costume changes, these and the props should be representational rather than specific. The overall effect is that of a dream.*

## Act 1

*The scene is an artist's studio. We see the outlines of a half-finished mural. Barely discernible are the figures of FRIDA KAHLO, LA CATRINA, HERNÁN CORTÉS, and SOR JUANA. There is a scaffolding of the kind used by artists to paint murals. Enter CHI-CHI holding a microphone.*

CHI-CHI

OK. Ready? I'll start the count. Five, four, three, two . . . Good evening. This is Chi-Chi Bautista reporting live from Alameda Park in downtown Mexico City, watching as they move the gigantic mural *Dreaming on a Sunday in the Alameda*. This dream of Maestro Diego Rivera is getting a new home where we'll soon witness the spirit and magic of this talented Mexican artist. And so, we invite you to come with us into this fantastic dream. This is Chi-Chi Batista for Channel 69. (*She fades out.*)

*Enter DIEGO RIVERA as a fifty-year-old man dressed in overalls, boots, and Stetson hat. He carries his brushes and work materials. Right behind is JOHNNY, carrying buckets of paint.*

DIEGO

(*Getting right to work, like a teacher instructing a pupil.*) I need more light in here! Start mixing the paints. I'll finish outlining the mural. And don't forget the special additive as prescribed by Dr. Atl. Why?

JOHNNY

So the paint will adhere to the wall.

DIEGO

Yes, for all time! It was Dr. Atl, that wise old sage, who found the secret of how the ancients painted the magnificent murals of Mexico. (*Starts outlining the mural.*) The Aztecs and Mayans made their murals last for centuries. It was a symbol of their power and the first public art in Mexico. And it was art for the masses, not for the bourgeois.

JOHNNY

But the mural is going up in the lobby of the Hotel del Prado. Isn't that a fancy hotel off Alameda Park?

DIEGO

Yes, but anyone can go there and see it, my boy. Come on, get busy, I want to finish this before (*Laughing.*) I die! (*They work in silence for a few beats, DIEGO outlining, JOHNNY mixing the different-colored paints.*)

JOHNNY

(*Showing him the paint.*) How's this, Maestro Rivera?

DIEGO

Darker, Yony. (*Pronouncing JOHNNY "Yony."*) Richer, brighter. My colors are the colors of the Aztec cosmos, brilliant, overpowering . . .

JOHNNY

Gaudy . . .

DIEGO

Yes, like Gaudí, the great plastic artist of Barcelona! Mix it well, my boy, mix it well. (*Smelling the paints.*) How I love the smell of paint!

JOHNNY

I'm ready, maestro.

DIEGO

Very well, Yony. Watch and learn the secrets of how to paint Mexican murals so you can take it back to your own country and apply the method there.

JOHNNY

Where shall we start?

DIEGO

With the Spanish, since one of the first viceroys founded the Paseo de la Alameda in 1592.

JOHNNY

What's the significance of this park, the Alameda?

DIEGO

It's the heart and lungs of the downtown area, like Central Park in New York City. Many things have happened here that affected Mexico City and, by extension, the entire country. (*Starting to apply paint.*) Now then, are you ready? Four centuries of Mexican history and five meters by fifteen meters of sheer genius on a wall!

JOHNNY

Are you going go start with the church?

DIEGO

Yes, the first notable institution founded by our noble Spanish conquerors was the . . . Inquisition!

JOHNNY

The Inquisition! (*Smoke starts spewing forth from the mural.*)

DIEGO

They burned the witches on the grounds of the convent. The Holy Inquisition torched sinners and damned souls unto everlasting hell! (*Spanish music of the sixteenth century begins to play.*)

JOHNNY

(*Running behind the mural.*) I smell smoke! Fire! (*Trying in vain to extinguish the blaze.*)

DIEGO

Can't you see the flames licking the sky, hear the crackling wood, smell the burning flesh?

MONK

(*A mysterious monk steps out of the mural and confronts DIEGO.*) Jesús, María y José! It's hot in there!

DIEGO

(*Startled.*) Who are you? How did you get in here?

MONK

(*Brushing off his robe.*) I don't know, but my clothes are on fire!

DIEGO

I see. Well, then, little monk, now you know how it feels to burn people alive!

MONK

I didn't burn anyone. What are you accusing me of?

DIEGO

What, you were "just following orders"?

MONK

It was Bishop Zumárraga who gave the commands.

DIEGO

Then what was it like to watch the beautiful Violante de Carvajal, daughter of a wealthy Monterrey family, burn to a crisp?

MONK

Well, it wasn't pleasant. (*Beat.*) She was accused of heresy.

DIEGO

But her only crime was that she was a Jew who practiced her religion in secret.

MONK

Who are you to judge me? And what makes you so high and mighty?

DIEGO

I am Diego Rivera, painter extraordinaire. It's all there in the windows of my Mexican memory. I hereby dedicate this mural, *Dreaming on a Sunday in the Alameda,* to the people of Mexico!

MONK

Don't be so presumptuous. Your ideas have nothing to do with reality anymore.

DIEGO

Insolent monk! You know damn well that without the struggle of the peasants and workers, my murals would not exist!

MONK

Is this the mural you're talking about? (*A shot of the mural Rivera painted at Rockefeller Center shines on a screen.*) The one you painted for Nelson Rockefeller in New York? (*DIEGO is taken aback by this; he says nothing.*) How much did he pay you? Twelve thousand dollars? Quite a tidy sum in 1933. Isn't that a contradiction, an avowed Marxist like yourself taking money from a Rockefeller?

DIEGO

I took his goddamn money. And painted a portrait of Lenin right in the middle of Rockefeller Center! He ordered me to erase it. I refused!

MONK

(*Accusing.*) You were also commissioned to paint murals for Henry Ford in Detroit, weren't you?

DIEGO

So what? I painted the workers and the wonderful machines they created. What are you anyway, an art critic? Go back to the mural, I've had enough of you! (*Trying to kick him.*) Get out of here with your silly questions and let me get to work!

MONK

All right, I'll go. Unless you want to say confession.

DIEGO

To hell with you! (*Mocking him.*) I don't believe in God! Do you hear me? God does not exist!

MONK

You're going to get in trouble saying things like that! (*The MONK disappears into the mural just as mysteriously as he entered.*)

DIEGO

One thing is certain, Johnny, when your creations start talking back, you are in trouble!

JOHNNY

The monk was from the sixteenth century. How did he know what was going on in the twentieth century?

DIEGO

(*Continuing to paint.*) One of the peculiarities of this creation is that it mixes time and space, so that the past and the present live side by side.

JOHNNY

Maestro, didn't you personally witness some of these things as a child? (*Music from the turn of the century starts to play.*)

DIEGO

When I was twelve I would come to Alameda Park on Sunday afternoon with my aunt . . . we would rent a bench and listen to the great bands play waltzes and military marches in the kiosk. This was around the turn of the nineteenth century, during the time of Porfirio Díaz.

JOHNNY

That's why you paint yourself as a child dressed in knickers and straw hat!

DIEGO

Surrounded by my family and friends. Now it's time to conjure up one of my loveliest creations, my greatest love, the beautiful and enchanting Frida Kahlo.

JOHNNY

She was *your* creation?

DIEGO

No, she is her own unique person. (*DIEGO starts painting the outline of FRIDA KAHLO dressed in Native attire.*) But she appeared to me as though in a dream. I was on a scaffold painting a mural in the college of San Ildefonso when a beautiful young girl shouted from below.

FRIDA

(*Coming to life.*) Diego! Diego Rivera!

DIEGO

(*Absorbed in his work, not looking at her.*) My lovely Fridita, my love child. Little did I know you would become the most important thing in my life!

FRIDA

Please stop painting, please, I have something I need to ask you.

DIEGO

(*Finally turning to her.*) Did I seduce you or you seduce me?

FRIDA

Are you so nearsighted that you don't recognize me when I'm standing right in front of you?

DIEGO

Excuse me? (*Taking a good long look at her.*) What magnificent eyebrows you have, like the wings of a blackbird!

FRIDA

I didn't come here to be made fun of. I have to earn my livelihood like everyone else.

DIEGO

I'm merely complimenting you.

FRIDA

I have three paintings I need judged professionally. I want to know if you think I'm a good enough artist. Will you look at them?

DIEGO

No, I don't have time right now. Go away! (*Turning back to his mural.*)

FRIDA

Diego, please!

DIEGO

(*Coming down from the scaffolding.*) Well, all right. I can't say "no" to a beautiful woman. (*Three self-portraits of FRIDA flash on the screen. He looks them over.*) Let's take a look.

FRIDA

These are three self-portraits.

DIEGO

Do you always paint yourself? It's rather risky, you know.

FRIDA

Why shouldn't I paint myself? I'm the person I know best!

DIEGO

Good answer! As for the paintings, they reveal an unusual energy of expression, precise delineation of character, and true severity.

FRIDA

Do you really think so, honestly?

DIEGO

They show none of the tricks in the name of originality that usually mark the work of ambitious beginners.

FRIDA

I'm very pleased. (*Beat.*) But I don't know whether to believe you.

DIEGO

Why not? Don't you trust my judgment?

FRIDA

They say that if a pretty girl asks you for something, you are ready to gush all over her. Be honest, do you really think I should keep painting?

DIEGO

By all means, no matter how difficult, you must continue.

FRIDA

I have other work at home. Could you come to my place next Sunday to see them? I live in Coyoacán with my parents.

DIEGO

I'd love to see more of your work! (*Exit FRIDA, as JOHNNY helps DIEGO remove his work clothes and put on a jacket.*) And so began my courtship of a girl young enough to be my own daughter.

JOHNNY

You were twice her age.

DIEGO

If it didn't bother her, it didn't bother me. (*JOHNNY hands DIEGO a bouquet of flowers.*) That Sunday I took a trolley all the way to Coyoacán and met her father, Don Guillermo.

DON GUILLERMO

(*Entering.*) I see you're interested in my daughter, Señor Rivera. Let me tell you, she had an accident a couple of years back, and she's in very delicate health.

DIEGO

Sir, I'm not marrying a horse, I'm marrying a woman.

DON GUILLERMO

I must warn you, she's extremely strong-willed and very intelligent. Which means she will surely drive you insane. Some do not think her particularly beautiful.

DIEGO

Sir, in my eyes, she is pretty, precious, and precocious. And I am resolved to marry her.

DON GUILLERMO

Very well, think it over, and if you still want to marry her, you have my permission.

DIEGO

It would be an honor to have Frida as my bride and you as my father-in-law.

DON GUILLERMO

She's a devil!

DIEGO

I know it.

DON GUILLERMO

Well, I warned you! (*DIEGO, FRIDA, and DON GUILLERMO pose as though in a wedding picture as JOHNNY takes the photo. Stage picture. Exit FRIDA and DON GUILLERMO.*)

DIEGO

(*Going back to his painting and thinking out loud.*) And now, it's time to paint something unpleasant, something repulsive. I'm going to paint that bastard Hernán Cortés. Yes, I'll paint him with his bloody hands gazing up to heaven asking God for forgiveness. (*Spanish music from the sixteenth century starts to play as DIEGO paints the outline of HERNÁN CORTÉS.*)

CORTÉS

(*Stepping out of the mural dressed like a Spanish captain of the sixteenth century.*) "Asking God for forgiveness"? For what?

DIEGO

(*With caution, this is a figure even more frightening than the MONK.*) For your crimes . . . against humanity.

CORTÉS

(*Noticing his hands covered with blood.*) Why are my hands bloody?

DIEGO

Because, uh, you're a bad . . . man.

CORTÉS

Why are there no statues of me in all of Mexico?

DIEGO

You . . . enslaved the Indians and raped our country.

CORTÉS

Nonsense! I brought the Indians up out of the muck of ignorance and superstition and into the light of civilization.

DIEGO

That's what Jason said to Medea.

CORTÉS

I'm the founder of this country. I'm practically your father, you ingrate!

DIEGO

No. My father wasn't a war criminal.

CORTÉS

Thou speakest sacrilege. (*Pointing to the screen.*) How could you paint me, the conqueror of Mexico, as a syphilitic on the walls of the National Palace?

DIEGO

Well, that's how they found your bones, rotten with syphilis and bowlegged.

CORTÉS

You would be bowlegged too if you were always striding atop a horse! Thou always sees the Indians as noble and good because thou paints propaganda!

DIEGO

Oh, go copulate with your mother! And gurgle with her menstrual juices!

CORTÉS

¡Me cago en la hostia! (*CORTÉS retreats back into the mural. DIEGO resumes painting.*)

JOHNNY

Well, maestro, your mural is certainly coming to life! (*DIEGO keeps painting.*) If you don't mind my asking, why do you hate the Spanish so much? Aren't you part Spanish?

DIEGO

Johnny, that's something only a gringo would ask!

JOHNNY

Sorry, sir, excuse me!

DIEGO

I may be part Spanish. But I'm also part Indian. And that side of me hates the Spanish with a passion. As a youth I turned my back on Mexico and went to live in Europe. I wanted to paint like them. I lived in Paris with a Russian woman for seven years and even had a child with her.

JOHNNY

What happened to them?

DIEGO

We were so poor we couldn't afford wood to warm our flat. The child died, and I left Europe.

JOHNNY

An omen?

DIEGO

Yes. When I returned to Mexico in 1921, you can't imagine my aesthetic joy. It was as if I had been reborn. All the colors were suddenly clearer, richer, brighter, and full of light. All at once I was in the very heart of the plastic arts, where colors and forms exist in their purest state. I saw a masterpiece in everything—the people, markets, festivals, in each face, in each child.

JOHNNY

Maestro, I think the secret of your best work is that it is Mexican.

DIEGO

He who hopes to be great must plant in his own soil. (*Beat. Looking at the mural.*) You know, I have a premonition that someone is missing from this mural! (*Beat.*) I'm hungry, let's go have some lunch. (*As DIEGO and JOHNNY exit, flutes and drums—indigenous music—play. Enter LA MALINCHE PUNK dressed in huipil, huaraches, black leather jacket, with purple spiked hair and a ring in her nose.*)

CORTÉS

(*Enter CORTÉS, slashing the air with his sword.*) Pyramids and volcanoes! Our journey between snowcapped mountains has carried us to the summit of glory! Mother Spain has come to give birth to a child called Mexico!

MALINCHE

You won't get far, dude. The roads that split the center of town divide the barrios of Quetzalcoatl and Tezcatlipoca.

CORTÉS

Pepsi . . . catlipoca . . . Coca . . . coatl . . . what strange names! The sword will disperse them in the name of the king! Besides, I've no fear of them, they think me a god!

MALINCHE

OK. Like, just don't get uptight when the shit comes down.

CORTÉS

Malinche, whose side are you on anyway? You're a Christian now!

MALINCHE

Look, I'm like, just a tourist guide, you know. You white boys are all alike. But just lay some dollars on me, and I'll show you whatever.

CORTÉS

And you do have a lot to show. You are one hot mamasota! (*Taking her by the waist.*)

MALINCHE

You know what, buddy, for me sex is like aerobics, just another way to get off. Like, if you're a virgin in Tenochtitlan you stand a good chance of getting sacrificed to the gods.

CORTÉS

Savages! I'll civilize them! (*Brandishing his sword.*)

MALINCHE

Oh yeah, they say you're a god, but wait until you see the Tiger or Eagle Warriors. Aren't you afraid?

CORTÉS

No! Go find my officers. Ask for my telescope so I can see the position of the enemy.

MALINCHE

Telescope? What's that?

CORTÉS

It's an instrument, a thing to help you see farther. Now, go, and be quick about it!

MALINCHE

(*Resentful.*) Huh, you think I'm your maid, or what? (*LA MALINCHE exits, then returns carrying an electric guitar.*) Wow!

CORTÉS

Hostia! How did I get mixed up with this dumb Indian wench?

MALINCHE

(*Throwing him the guitar.*) Here's your "thing"!

CORTÉS

What the hell am I supposed to do with this? (*Trying to see through the guitar.*)

MALINCHE

I don't know, you invented it.

CORTÉS

(*Looking through his instrument.*) What's this? Nacos! Nacos and tacos! Jesus, there's too many Indios. We'll never be able to conquer them all. (*He inadvertently starts to play the guitar.*) Wow, too much!

MALINCHE

(*Seeing something in the distance.*) Wait a minute, a procession appears in the distance, a majestic figure on a carriage!

CORTÉS

Could it be Moco-zuma himself?

MALINCHE

No, it's not Moctezuma, it's the American ambassador, Meeeeester Black Bridge.

CORTÉS

Shit! Pinche gringos. Are they here already? Why, we haven't even conquered this place!

MALINCHE

That's right, you better learn English, you'll be rapping it before long. Look, right next to the ambassador is a boss of the ruling party. He's a prick, but if you give him a mordida, he'll let you put up a chain of taco stands.

CORTÉS

To hell with taco stands! (*Starting to play again.*) I want gold, nothing but gold, because I have a pain in my heart that can be cured by gold and only gold! (*Playing a nice riff, LA MALINCHE sways to and fro.*) Or perhaps platinum will do! Yes! We shall found the beautiful city of Tele-nacho-landia!

MALINCHE

Tenochtitlan, buddy, the belly button of the pale moon.

CORTÉS

Call it what you want. We'll impose a new order. Down with the old pagan ways. Down with "La Cucaracha" and the mambo and the tango! Up with rock'n'roll, punk, and techno-banda! (*Pulling a bottle of Coke out of his coat and giving it to her.*) Here!

MALINCHE

(*Showing the audience the label.*) Coca-Cola! (*Drinks it.*) I like it!

CORTÉS

(*Accompanying himself on the guitar. MALINCHE sucks on the Coke bottle and dances.*)
    El Conquistador
    Landed on the shore
    Broke down the front door
    El Conquistador
    Fifteen and nineteen
    Landed in blue jeans
    It's not what it seems
    Fifteen and nineteen.

MALINCHE

(*Singing a verse.*)
    Yo soy La Malinche
    Say I am a pinche
    Made love to the rinche
    Yo soy La Malinche
    Say I'm La Chingada
    Me lleva la fregada!
    They act like I got sida
    I'm not a vendida!

(*Fade out on CORTÉS and LA MALINCHE.*)

BLONDIE

(*Enter BLONDIE with her doll.*) This is my doll, my friend, my gold, my silver. This is my pillow, my day, my night, my star. This is my doll. My present, my pal. And when I go to the Alameda with my father, she comes with me. Because this lovely doll is my friend, my gold, my silver, my pillow, my day, my night, my star. And I am here in this famous mural, in the mural of this famous artist. And I am part of a dream, a lovely dream that is as beautiful as my doll, my friend, my gold, my silver, my pillow, my day, my night, my star. (*She exits.*)

DIEGO

(*Entering with JOHNNY.*) You know something Johnny, I don't remember painting La Malinche . . . Punk . . . did you say?

JOHNNY

Yes, one of the many dynamic movements of the late twentieth century.

DIEGO

It's rather interesting, actually. It has a nihilistic quality I find refreshing. But where did she come from? She wasn't in my mural.

JOHNNY

I don't know, perhaps she's haunting you maestro!

DIEGO

I see. (*They start setting up for the next scene.*) Now, then, whom shall I paint next?

JOHNNY

May I suggest Sor Juana Inés de la Cruz, the most notable female poet of New Spain during the colonial period.

DIEGO

Also known as the Tenth Muse! You're going to help me out by posing as the tavern owner, a debased voluptuary. Even though you're not the type.

JOHNNY

I'll do my best, sir.

DIEGO

Well, try and get into character.

JOHNNY

(*Trying to get into character.*) I'm thinking of what the great Dante once said, or was it Chaucer, "To the church with the saints, but to the inn with the gluttons!"

DIEGO

My sentiments exactly. Do you know that, as students, we used to purchase cadavers from the city morgue and lived on this cannibal diet for two months!

JOHNNY

Maestro, you're pulling my leg!

DIEGO

Why no, the Aztecs ate human flesh. They even made tamales of their sacrificial victims.

JOHNNY

Is this another of your tall tales, your propensity to spin myths of maniacal proportions?

DIEGO

What I like best are the legs and breasts of women, for as in other animals, these are delicacies. I also enjoy young women's tongues. Best of all, however, I relish women's brains!

JOHNNY

(*Getting into the act.*) Then I'll make a daily special: "Roasted Feminist Thighs"! "Stuffed Breasts in Mole"! "Brains de la femme ala vinaigrette"!

DIEGO

Say, you are getting into the role! (*Enter CORTÉS. He sits at another table. He and DIEGO glare at each other.*) What are you looking at?

CORTÉS

Bartender, two bottles of wine from Rioja, please. One for me and one for my son, the fat boy sitting over there.

DIEGO

(*Threatening.*) If you keep fucking with me, I'm going to erase you from the mural! (*CORTÉS backs off and makes apologetic gestures. Enter SOR JUANA INEZ DE LA CRUZ dressed in a nun's habit of the sixteenth century. They all stare at her with obvious lust in their eyes.*)

SOR JUANA

I feel a searing fire. Whose eyes look at me with desire?

DIEGO

Little mother, what can I do for you? (*Taking her hand.*)

SOR JUANA

I seek escape from this mortal coil. Know ye not where I may find that soil?

DIEGO

(*Mimicking her.*) Come, come, don't frown, I'll fix you a potion to calm you down.

SOR JUANA

Somewhere in this sordid sphere, I must find truth or die, I fear.

DIEGO

(*Preparing her a drink and talking to himself.*) Oh boy, we got a hot one here. I'll fix her a Mickey Finn and help her discover mortal sin!

CORTÉS

(*Sauntering up to the her, drink in hand.*) Doest thou study or doest thou workest?

SOR JUANA

Until today when I left my cell, my only succor was spiritual.

JOHNNY

(*Standing between her and CORTÉS.*) Excuse me sir, can't you see she's not interested in the material?

CORTÉS

(*Taking SOR JUANA by the arm and leading her away from the others.*) Come, come, there's too many "flies" on the bar. (*Serving her.*) Drink up, little nun, I promise it'll be a great deal of fun!

SOR JUANA

(*Drinking.*) Doest thou think this libation will cure all my ills? If so, then I'll drinkest my fill!

CORTÉS

Over the convent's walls you leap . . . (*Putting his hand on her leg. She recoils at his touch.*) How do you mean to earn your keep?

SOR JUANA

(*Giving CORTÉS a vicious karate kick in the private parts.*) My source of employ is my pen. Do you have a task of that kind herein? (*As CORTÉS writhes on the floor in pain.*)

CORTÉS

It's just that we don't need any secretaries right now. And that long skirt, it's going to have to be shorter to attract the clientele. You must have very strong legs to kick that hard.

DIEGO

Do you mind if I take a look? (*Trying to lift up her skirt, she threatens to kick DIEGO. He backs off.*) Don't you have any other "talents"?

SOR JUANA

Sonnets, tercetes, cuartets . . .

DIEGO

You are operatically inclined! To dance a jig or a cancan do you mind?

SOR JUANA

Of exotic dances I no not, but give me a story, a song, or a plot.

CORTÉS

Surely you know how to dance the mambo!

SOR JUANA

No, not even the tango.

CORTÉS

Who art thou? What's they name?

SOR JUANA

Like simple fauna, my name is Juana.

JOHNNY

Caballero, this is Sor Juana. She was a champion of women's rights in the eighteenth century.

CORTÉS

(*Trying to be sincere.*) Wonderful. I like independent women. They make me feel "whole."

SOR JUANA

(*Somewhat frightened.*) This has got me so confused! One moment a mural, the next "The Lost Muse"!

DIEGO

Splendid, splendid! And now ladies and gentlemen, "The Lost Muse" announces that Sor Juanita will be our official dancer! Yes, yes, you must dance, I insist! Her first dance will be the . . .

SOR JUANA

Well, well, all right! Uh, the . . . flamenco!

CORTÉS

¡Olé! ¡Olé! ¡El flamenco! (*Flamenco music is heard. CORTÉS becomes very emotional and starts clapping. SOR JUANA climbs up on a table, raises her skirt, and starts dancing. All at once FRIDA enters. The music and dancing stop.*)

FRIDA

What's this? A Buñuel film?

DIEGO

Sugar plum! I was merely sketching Sor Juanita and . . .

FRIDA

Well, instead of wasting your time in this hole in the wall, why don't you go and finish your murals in the National Palace. Have you heard the joke? "Twenty years and Diego still hasn't finished painting the stairwell!" (*As FRIDA starts to push DIEGO out.*)

CORTÉS

(*Mocking DIEGO.*) Henpecked! Show her who has the huevos! (*Enter LA MALINCHE.*)

MALINCHE

(*To CORTÉS.*) Let's go you good for nothing! (*Grabbing CORTÉS by the ear.*) Don't you hear poor little Martincito bawling while you drink with your cronies? (*They exit.*)

FRIDA

(*To SOR JUANA.*) Well, Sor Juana. Let's you and I sit down and have a drink. (*FRIDA motions to JOHNNY who serves them. FRIDA flirts with him.*) What a handsome young man!

SOR JUANA

I don't know what came over me. I've never been so insulted and humiliated! Dancing the flamenco and having me speak in doggerel!

FRIDA

I'm afraid it's Diego's dream, not mine.

SOR JUANA

Men are such mules, how can you stand them! That's why I went into the convent.

FRIDA

I suppose you want to hear a very feminist report about Diego, full of derogatory gossip and indecent revelations.

SOR JUANA

Is it true he goes out with other women, right under your very nose?

FRIDA

How could I love a man who wasn't attractive to other women?

SOR JUANA

And that disgusting Cortés! (*Mimicking him.*) "Doest thou study or doest thou workest"! (*She and FRIDA laugh and toast to each other.*)

FRIDA

You know, I drink to drown my sorrows, but the damned things have learned to swim! (*Lights fade on FRIDA and SOR JUANA.*)

DIEGO

(*Entering with JOHNNY.*) Well Yony, see how it works? The mural is made up of a series of frames that, when put all together, tell the story of the Alameda. Now I'm going to paint one of my favorite scenes. A peasant family was trying to get into the park when they were stopped by a gendarme. (*DIEGO sketches the outlines of LA YERBERA, as JOHNNY sets up for the next scene.*)

*The scene is Alameda Park. Enter LA YERBERA, who is arguing with the POLICÍA.*

POLICÍA

Come on, old mother, you have to move on.

YERBERA

But why, my son, this is where I always sell my herbs.

POLICÍA

Rules are rules. The boss will have my head.

YERBERA

If you don't let me be, I'll put a spell on you!

POLICÍA

At least go back there where you won't be seen!

YERBERA

Then how will people know I'm here? (*Beat.*) My son, I see you are sad, what ails you?

POLICÍA

My heart is hurting, old mother.

YERBERA

What happened?

POLICÍA

I fought with my woman and hit her. She left me and took our daughter. It was my fault. I wish they would come back to me!

YERBERA

Let me help you, I see that you have a good heart. I have a magic potion that will bring them back. (*They go off to the side discussing.*)

*Enter a well-dressed bourgeois GENTLEMEN carrying a newspaper. With him is his ten-year-old daughter. She is blond and blue-eyed. She carries a purse, along with a blue-eyed and blond-haired doll.*

GENTLEMAN

Go ahead, Beatriz, go play while I read the newspaper.

BLONDIE

Why don't you play with me, Papi?

GENTLEMAN

Because I have to read the paper. Play with your new doll. And don't get your dress dirty! (*Downcast, the girl stands off to the side. Enter a dark-complexioned girl dressed in rebozo and huaraches.*)

MORENA

(*To BLONDIE.*) What a pretty doll.

BLONDIE

Yes, she is beautiful isn't she?

MORENA

Can I touch her?

BLONDIE

Sure. Feel her blond hair.

MORENA

You know, she looks a little like you. Except her skin is whiter.

BLONDIE

She's a gringa. My father got her on a business trip in the United States. Her name is Beti, like me. (*Giving MORENA the doll.*) Go on, you can hold her. What's your name?

MORENA

Guadalupe. Lupe for short.

BLONDIE

Our maid is named Guadalupe. She lives in Tepeyac, where the Virgin of Guadalupe appeared to Juan Diego. My mother thinks this is very funny. (*She giggles.*) Would you like to play "cocktails"?

MORENA

"Cocktails"?

BLONDIE

Yes, like adults. We can pretend to get drunk and talk real loud. (She pulls out three champagne glasses from her purse and places them on a bench.) One for you, one for me, and one for Beti. (Pulls out a small champagne bottle from the purse.) Here's the bubbly! (Serving everyone.) Careful, don't spill it! Now then! Bottoms up!

MORENA

¡Salud!

BLONDIE

Here's looking at you!

MORENA

Cheers! (*They drink.*)

BLONDIE

I like a good champagne, don't you?

MORENA

I think I'm getting drunk. (*Beat.*) Is this all they do at cocktails?

BLONDIE

Yes, they also gossip. Lots of gossip. (*As the champagne begins to go to her head.*) Let's do it. I'll go first. (*Beat.*) Guadalupe doesn't wear underwear!

MORENA

Yes, I do!

BLONDIE

Not you, silly, the other Guadalupe! Now it's Beti's turn. (*Looking at her father to see if he is listening. She takes the doll and makes her "speak."*) I saw Daddy kissing the maid! (*The father overhears this and frowns.*)

MORENA

Really? What a whopper!

BLONDIE

Now it's your turn. Tell us a real juicy one!

MORENA

Well, let's see. Here goes. The maid is going to have a baby. And the father isn't the milkman!

BLONDIE

Who is the father?

MORENA

Can't you guess? (*They both look over at the father, who stands up, infuriated.*) It ain't Granny Goose! (*The father walks over to his daughter, picks up her things, takes her by the hand, and sits her down on his bench.*)

BLONDIE

But I want to play with my friend!

GENTLEMAN

You stay here! (*Going over to the POLICÍA.*) ¡Policía!

POLICÍA

¿Sí señor?

GENTLEMAN

Get that smelly little girl out of here!

POLICÍA

Is there some kind of problem, sir?

GENTLEMAN

She's saying nasty things to my daughter. I'm sure she has fleas and God knows what else. (*The policeman nods his head and tips his hat. The father goes back and sits down at the bench with BLONDIE.*)

POLICÍA

(*Walking over to MORENA.*) Little girl, I'm afraid you're going to have to leave the park.

MORENA

What for, I didn't do anything!

POLICÍA

Don't argue with me. You know you're not supposed to be here.

MORENA

I just want to play with my friend!

YERBERA

(*Stepping in between them.*) Leave her alone!

POLICÍA

(*To YERBERA.*) You keep out of this. (*Grabbing MORENA.*) He's right, you do smell! Go on, or I'll kick you out by the seat of your pants!

MORENA

(*Starting to cry.*) Leave me alone, let me go!

YERBERA

Stop, what are you doing?

POLICÍA

You know this park is reserved only for the better classes. If the gentleman says the girl is bothering them, she has to go. Matter of fact, so do you!

YERBERA

Oh yes, look at you. I suppose you think you're one of the "better classes"! One of the "European" people!

POLICÍA

I'm only doing my job!

YERBERA

Don't you see. She could be your daughter. (*She throws some seeds over his head. Pre-Columbian flutes and drums are heard.*)

POLICÍA

What is going on here?

YERBERA

Listen, my son, do you hear something?

POLICÍA

Where's that music coming from?

YERBERA

From the heart, the soul, your Mexican soul. That girl is your daughter!

POLICÍA

Are you putting a spell on me?

YERBERA

Don't you know who you are? (*The POLICÍA is in a kind of trance.*) You are Cuauhtemoc, the last of the Aztec warrior kings.

POLICÍA

No I'm not, my name is Juan.

YERBERA

(*Unbuttoning his tunic.*) Look underneath the uniform, Cuauhtemoc, what do you see? (*She reveals the feathers on his chest.*)

POLICÍA

Feathers! ¡Ah, chihuahua! (*He takes off his uniform. Underneath, the POLICÍA is dressed like an Aztec warrior.*)

YERBERA

And do you know who he is? (*They both cross over to the bench where the man is sitting. MORENA takes the opportunity to escape and join BLONDIE.*)

POLICÍA

Excuse me, do you mind showing me your identification?

GENTLEMAN

What for? And who's this woman?

POLICÍA

Your identification, please.

GENTLEMAN

You know, I could have your job for this! (*Giving him his ID.*)

POLICÍA

So, your name is Cortés, eh?

GENTLEMAN

Yes, Alejandro Cortés! You'll remember that name!

YERBERA

You were sleeping with the maid, weren't you? And you got her pregnant!

GENTLEMAN

What business is it of yours?

POLICÍA

You did, didn't you? You refused to recognize the child as your own and failed to pay for the child's support! Let's go, I'm taking you in!

GENTLEMAN

What for? Are you crazy? What's the charge?

POLICÍA

(*Grabbing him.*) Rape! Genocide!

GENTLEMAN

Genocide! (*Pulling out a sword.*) Stupid Indian! I'll cut your head off!

POLICÍA

(*Pulling out a club like the kind used by the Aztecs.*) And I'll rip your heart out! (*CORTÉS and Cuauhtemoc start fighting.*)

YERBERA

(*Helping Cuauhtemoc.*) Death to the Gachupines! ¡Que Viva Benito Juárez! ¡Que Viva La Virgen de Guadalupe! (*CORTÉS exits with LA YERBERA and POLICÍA in hot pursuit. MORENA and the blond girl continue playing, oblivious to everything. Slow fade.*)

*The next scene is FRIDA's house. DIEGO is painting names of women on the walls. Enter JOHNNY.*

JOHNNY

I see it now, maestro, everyone is dreaming! The Indian family dreaming of overthrowing their colonizers. Cortés dreaming of redemption, perhaps?

DIEGO

That's right, Johnny. What are you dreaming about?

JOHNNY

I don't know. I'm not in the mural! (*Noticing what DIEGO is painting.*) Maestro, why are you painting the names of all these women on the walls?

DIEGO

Because Frida said she wanted to know the names of all the women I slept with.

JOHNNY

(*Reading out loud.*) "All of these women have slept with me, with my guts and this poor tired body that sustains itself through human flesh. Ángela, Lupe, Tina, Iris, Rosa, Flor, Petunia"! Oh, my God, here she comes. I better go! (*JOHNNY exits.*)

FRIDA

(*Entering. Angry but in control.*) I risked my life three times to have your baby. I suffered a torturous miscarriage in Detroit. For what?

DIEGO

Never before has a woman like you put such agonized poetry on canvas as you have. I stand humbled before you!

FRIDA

So that's how you repay me! (*Pointing to the walls.*) By painting this on the walls and ceiling of my home!

DIEGO

(*Trying to make light of it.*) Each women was but a scale to reach your heights. (*Seriously.*) Frida, you know my horrible history.

FRIDA

Don't make fun of me! It's the same tired old song that you sang to all the others.

DIEGO

Yes, but the song varies. Sometimes I sing in alto . . . sometimes I sing in bass.

FRIDA

You're a monster, Diego.

DIEGO

Cannibal. And I don't have space to put all the rest.

FRIDA

Why do you humiliate me like this?

DIEGO

I'm just trying to be honest. You said you wanted to know, "so there would be no more surprises."

FRIDA

Why this voracious, self-destructive lust for women?

DIEGO

Frida, I told you. It gives me pleasure, sensation, exaltation! Besides, you don't mind my infidelity as much as my choice of women.

FRIDA

Sluts.

DIEGO

But by letting you draw the line, do I not circumscribe my own freedom? Frida, I am weak. They come looking for me! You know full well that women seek fame. "I slept with Diego Rivera. I fornicated with a genius!"

FRIDA

Now you're going to say that's why I married you!

DIEGO

No. I married you. I was the one who wanted to be the husband of Frida Kahlo.

FRIDA

Then act like it! Goddamn it! (*She walks away. SOR JUANA enters and sits down next to her.*)

JOHNNY

(*Going to DIEGO and wiping Diego's face with a towel, as though in a boxing match.*) I think you've got her on the run, sir. She's astounded by your lack of duplicity and your total candor!

DIEGO

I'm going to build two homes for us, side by side. She'll have her studio and living quarters. I'll have my studio and living quarters. A passageway will connect both houses. When we want to be together, we will. When we don't, we won't!

JOHNNY

A perfect way to ensure domestic tranquility.

FRIDA

(*To SOR JUANA as she prepares Frida for the next "round."*) He wants his own "space" as he calls it, so he can entertain the gringa "art aficionados" who come to visit him.

SOR JUANA

How you can put up with a marriage that causes you so much pain?

FRIDA

That's how he is, and that's how I love him. I cannot love him for what he is not!

SOR JUANA

At least tell him you want an "open marriage." See how that grabs him!

DIEGO

(*Upon hearing this, DIEGO stands up, ready to fight.*) Open marriage, you want to see other men?

SOR JUANA

And other women as well!

FRIDA

(*Throwing the first punch.*) What's good for the gander is good for the goose! I'm going to have an affair with Leon Trotsky!

DIEGO

Leon Trotsky, that old billy goat!

FRIDA

I'll do it out of . . . solidarity. He's one of the greatest revolutionaries of our time!

JOHNNY

You've no choice, sir, she has you by the cojones. If you back down you'll lose face. Pull a macho trip, she'll accuse you of having double standards.

DIEGO

(*Retreating, on his "bicycle."*) All right, I agree to an open marriage. End of discussion. Now I have to go and finish painting my mural.

SOR JUANA

(*Pulling no punches.*) Wait, Diego, there's one more name you forgot to add to your list!

DIEGO

Who's that?

SOR JUANA

Cristina!

FRIDA

Cristina! My sister! (*She drops to the floor on one knee.*) My own sister!

SOR JUANA

A low blow! (*JOHNNY starts the "count."*)

FRIDA

Diego, how could you?

DIEGO

I was alone, Frida, sad and depressed. You were out of the city. It just happened!

FRIDA

Like the streetcar that cracked my spine, broke me apart, my backbone slowing disintegrating . . . you're killing me! (*FRIDA is saved by the bell as it rings. She goes and sits down in her corner.*)

SOR JUANA
>You have to leave him.

DIEGO
>(*Going to his corner.*) My God, am I a victim of my own depraved appetites? It seems like the more I love a woman, the more I want to hurt her. Frida is only the latest victim of this disgusting trait.

JOHNNY
>Sir, don't worry, she'll be back . . . for the rematch!

FRIDA
>I'm leaving you, Diego. I'm going to live by myself and have all the affairs I want!

DIEGO
>Good-bye. I'm going to miss you, Fridita.

FRIDA
>You'll never find another like me, sapo rana.

DIEGO
>I know that, amaranth flower. (*Meeting in the middle of the ring, both are exhausted.*)

FRIDA
>In your mural, you painted me holding the symbol of yin-yang. Why?

DIEGO
>Because two halves make a whole, and without you I am incomplete.

FRIDA
>And what are you dreaming of?

DIEGO
>Of love par excellence personified by you!

FRIDA
>Will you ever change?

DIEGO
>I doubt it. (Kissing her.) I doubt it. (Blackout.)

JOHNNY
>(*Like an announcer.*) The fight has been declared . . . a draw! (*JOHNNY holds up DIEGO's arm, SOR JUANA holds up FRIDA's arm. Blackout.*)

# End Act 1

La Malinche consoles Hernán Cortés after Spanish forces suffer a defeat during "La Noche Triste" (The Sad Night). Arizona Theatre Company production of *La Malinche*, Tucson and Phoenix, 1997.

La Malinche, her servant, and La Llorona (The Weeping Woman) plot against the Spanish. Arizona Theatre Company production of *La Malinche*, Tucson and Phoenix, 1997.

La Malinche warns her son, Martín, not to touch the presents meant for Cortés' bride-to-be. Arizona Theatre Company production of *La Malinche*, Tucson and Phoenix, 1997.

The Spanish avarice for gold will be the lure by which La Malinche gets her revenge. Arizona Theatre Company production of *La Malinche*, Tucson and Phoenix, 1997.

La Malinche "punk" and a conquistador rock star contemplate the taking of Tenochitlan. Theatre Department, University of California, Riverside, production of *Dreaming on a Sunday in the Alameda*, 1992.

Television host Chi-Chi introduces dictator Porfirio Díaz to an adoring public. Theatre Department, University of California, Riverside, production of *Dreaming on a Sunday in the Alameda*, 1992.

Frida Kahlo, Sor Juana, and La Malinche "punk" confront artist Diego Rivera.
Theatre Department, University of California, Riverside, production of
*Dreaming on a Sunday in the Alameda*, 1992.

Diego Rivera admires La Catrina (Lady Death). Theatre Department, University of California, Riverside, production of *Dreaming on a Sunday in the Alameda*, 1992.

Las mujeres hang their laundry in the Mexican part of Zinc Town. University of Wisconsin, School of Music, production of *Esperanza*, Madison, 2000.

Ramón and a pregnant Esperanza wonder what kind of world their child will live in. University of Wisconsin, School of Music, production of *Esperanza*, Madison, 2000.

Ramón and Vicente belatedly agree that "hot water and sanitation should have been one of the union's demands." University of Wisconsin, School of Music, production of *Esperanza*, Madison, 2000.

Esperanza leads the women in defying the sheriff's attempted eviction of Zinc Town. University of Wisconsin, School of Music, production of *Esperanza*, Madison, 2000.

# Act 2

*The set has become magically transformed into a television studio.*
*CORTÉS enters, dressed like a sleazy Latin American dictator, with LA*
*MALINCHE.*

CORTÉS

> I think we've got him. I'm going to expose him for the fraud that he
> is.

MALINCHE

> Like his commissions from the government are a kind of mordida—
> letting him paint some hammer and sickles in public buildings
> makes the government look hip.

CORTÉS

> Meanwhile he goes around making tons of money painting portraits
> of the rich and famous.

MALINCHE

> He also did a gig for the American ambassador, remember him? He
> painted murals on the Palace of Cortés! Your palace, dude, in
> Cuernavaca!

CORTÉS

> What! His murals on the walls of my palace! I'll kill him. Oh God,
> the humiliation of it all. The conqueror of Mexico and what do I
> have to show for it? Shhhh, here he comes! (*Applause and music are*
> *heard in the background.*) What's all that noise?

MALINCHE

> It's like the *Tonight Show*, dude, and you're the special guest!

CORTÉS

> No! Is that why I'm dressed like a tinhorn dictator?

MALINCHE

> Yes! You're playing Porfirio Díaz, the man who ruled Mexico for
> thirty years! And the show is about to start!

CORTÉS

> No, I refuse to go on!

DIEGO

> (*Entering and holding a pistol.*) Shut up! This is my dream! We do
> what I say! (*LA MALINCHE sits with the audience and the program*

Buenas Noches, Siiiiiii *begins. Enter CHI-CHI BATISTA in a low-cut sequined dress. There are strobe lights, cameras, and music that makes you want to tap your feet.*)

CHI-CHI

Good evening, my friends. Welcome to *Buenas Noches, Siiiiiii!*

CHORUS

Siiiiiii!

CHI-CHI

Here in the studio is a replica of Diego Rivera's mural *Dreaming on a Sunday in the Alameda.* (*A slide of the mural shines on a screen.*) And here to talk to us about this wonderful mural and other things is none other than . . . oh, I am so thrilled . . . (*She makes a phalangist salute.*) With us, live in a broadcast beamed to the five continents and into intergalactic space . . . with us the vital king of the Mechicas . . . emperor of the Chilangos . . . Generalíssimo Porfirio Díaz!

CHORUS

Siiiiiii! (*Cheers, cries, mayhem. Enter DON PORFIS like a rock star dressed in a tuxedo with cape. DIEGO puts on some sunglasses and becomes his bodyguard, attending to him throughout the broadcast.*)

PORFIS

(*Aside to DIEGO.*) I feel like a fool in this monkey suit! (*DIEGO pushes him down onto the seat.*)

CHI-CHI

(*Flirting with him.*) Please sit down, Señor Presidente. I am so filled with emotion. Oh, my goodness, here is the big boss, the pres Don Porfis himself. How you doing? What's happening?

PORFIS

(*PORFIS is unsure of what to say, so DIEGO whispers in his ear.*) Uh, well, my much esteemed and gorgeous Chi-Chi. (*DIEGO whispers in his ear again.*) I'm retired. I've been visiting people all over the world. I spent time with Mussolini in Italy, Franco in Spain, Pinochet in Chile, Ronnie Reagan in Santa Barbara. And now I'm back in Mexico!

CHI-CHI

You're immortal! You never die! (*She kisses him passionately on the lips.*) What would you do if you were running the country again, generalíssimo, how would you handle the problem of the foreign debt?

PORFIS

Ah . . . (*DIEGO cues him.*) We could sell . . . some paintings by Orozco or Siqueiros. Mexico exports its art! (*Getting into the act and gesturing to DIEGO.*) Write that down, young man. And bring me a rum and Coke, plenty of ice. (*DIEGO fetches him a drink, then applies some makeup on his face.*) We also have a lot of archaeological treasures, thousands of pyramids, tons of Olmec heads.

CHI-CHI

Why not? The government is selling the telephone company, the copper mines! Why not art?

PORFIS

Exactly. That way we could borrow more. You see, the way to stay out of debt is . . . to borrow!

CHI-CHI

You are a genius, Don Porfis. We need men like you back in power. Let's talk about the ecology. What are we going to do? They're cutting down all our trees.

PORFIS

But we need the toothpicks for the olives in the martinis!

CHI-CHI

How could you solve the problem of the severe water shortage?

PORFIS

By drinking more Coca-Cola! Do you know that we Mexicans drink more Coca-Cola than any other people on earth? (*Ordering DIEGO around, enjoying his power.*) Young man, another drink please! (*DIEGO puts more makeup on him.*) These television lights are really hot, aren't they? How do you hold up so well, my Chi-Chi? You always have such a radiant smile on your face, and your makeup never runs.

CHI-CHI

It's permanently painted on, Don Porfis, merely a little trade secret. Here's a toughie for you. You know that Mexico City has the world's worst air pollution?

PORFIS

But I have a solution. A giant turbine. A huge fan that will blow all the bad air away!

CHI-CHI

Blow it where? Into the countryside?

PORFIS

Exactly. Each big city could have its own giant fan that would blow bad air into the rural areas where there is plenty of clean air.

CHI-CHI

We could export this technology to places like Los Angeles!

PORFIS

I would also decree a "One Day without Air" program. You know, like the scheme with the automobiles, "One Day without a Car."

CHI-CHI

Uh-huh! But what if that doesn't work?

PORFIS

We start charging for clean air.

CHI-CHI

What a novel idea! You mean charge the polluters for fouling the air?

PORFIS

No, charge the citizens a couple of pesos a snort for clean mobile air-units.

CHI-CHI

Don Porfis, how would you solve unemployment?

PORFIS

"One Day without Work."

CHI-CHI

Hunger?

PORFIS

"One Day without Tacos." Actually, I have a plan to eliminate contaminated air, unemployment, and hunger in one fell swoop!

CHI-CHI

(*To the audience, as she hugs DON PORFIS.*) My God, they don't make men like this anymore! Generalíssimo, tell us about your plan to eliminate bad air, unemployment, and hunger!

PORFIS

First, we take all the engines out of the automobiles and stop building cars with engines.

CHI-CHI

Right, because that's what causes the contamination.

PORFIS

Cars will be considerably lighter. We'll rig up harnesses so cars can be pulled by men, women, or children. That puts people to work. Depending upon how fast you want to go, you hire a few drivers for the city and a whole gang for the freeway.

CHI-CHI

And instead of gasoline, you just stop off at a few taco stands and feed the people!

PORFIS

Right, you just have to watch out for the exhaust fumes caused by the excess of beans! (*Waving his hand in front of his face.*)

CHI-CHI

You should be nominated for the Noble Peace (*Pronounced "piss."*) Prize.

PORFIS

But let's not talk about these things anymore, my dear Chi-Chi. Let us speak of life, love, wine, and song. (*To DIEGO.*) Young man, another drink! (*DIEGO gives DON PORFIS the entire bottle and applies more makeup on him.*)

CHI-CHI

Well, then, why don't you sing us a song. Come on!

PORFIS

No, no, no . . .

AUDIENCE

Siiiiiiiii!

PORFIS

But I only know one song!

CHI-CHI

The same one you've been singing for one hundred years!

PORFIS

(*Getting into the act.*) Do you know that Diego Rivera, although somewhat of an agitator and Red, was a great chef? He used to serve quesadillas made of human meat!

CHI-CHI

Don Porfis, how revolting!

PORFIS

It's the secret of my longevity. How do you think I've managed to stay fit all these years? Why, I've gorged on tamales of Huitzilopochtli!

DIEGO

(*Aside to the audience.*) I think I created a monster! (*He exits.*)

PORFIS

(*As an orchestra plays.*) Estos huaraches que tengo yo
Son de tu abuela que se murió (*He keeps uttering the doggerel, chasing after CHI-CHI, tickling her and feeling her up.*)
These huaraches that I have on
Belonged to grandma who's dead and gone

CHI-CHI

(*Giving herself over to him.*) ¡Ohhhh síiiiii!

PORFIS

(*Kissing her.*) Do you know what my Chi-Chi, I have a wonderful idea. How would you like to see a melodrama, a soap opera from the life of Diego Rivera?

CHI-CHI

Really! Where?

PORFIS

Right here in the next studio.

CHI-CHI

(*Getting ready to participate.*) I love it!

PORFIS

The scene is a working-class bar Diego liked to frequent. (*Enter FRIDA, who sets up the next scene.*) It is late at night, and the bar is already closed. Frida is drinking pulque with Sor Juanita.

CHI-CHI

Oh! Can I play Sor Juanita? She's so in vogue.

PORFIS

Of course my dear Chi-Chi, you're made for the part. (*Exits PORFIS.*)

FRIDA

(*With SOR JUANA, waxing nostalgic.*) I suffered two serious accidents in my life. One in which a streetcar ran over me and broke my spine, and the other when I married Diego Rivera!

SOR JUANA

You have to get over this infatuation with Diego, it's very self-destructive.

FRIDA

I cannot speak of Diego as my husband because that term, when applied to him, is absurd. He never has been, nor will he ever be, anyone's husband.

SOR JUANA

He'll never grow up, he's a brat, a big baby.

FRIDA

I also cannot speak of him as my lover because, to me, he transcends by far the domain of sex. And if I attempt to speak of his soul, I'll only end up by painting my own emotions.

SOR JUANA

You must rid yourself of him!

FRIDA

But the banks of a river do not suffer because they let the river overflow, or the earth because of the rains, or the atom for letting its energy escape. (*There is a knock on the door. Enter LA MALINCHE with a knife in her hand.*)

MALINCHE

(*Melodramatically.*) Frida, just give me the word, and I'll kill Diego Rivera!

SOR JUANA

Malinche, why do you hate him so much?

MALINCHE

Because he didn't paint me in the mural!

FRIDA

You just don't understand him, Malinche. To Diego, painting is every-thing. He spends between twelve and eighteen hours a day painting. He cannot lead a normal life. He doesn't have time to think of his actions as being moral, amoral, or immoral.

*A knock on the door is heard.*

MALINCHE

How lovely, here we are, three intelligent women, spending our time talking about a stupid man! (*A loud knock is heard. She looks through the peephole.*) It's him! What should I do?

FRIDA

Let him in!

SOR JUANA

No! (*LA MALINCHE whispers in SOR JUANA's ear. She has a plan. LA MALINCHE opens the door.*)

DIEGO

(*Entering, seeing himself outnumbered.*) Oh, Frida, I didn't know the three of you were having a little feminist meeting. I'll come back another time when we can talk in private. (*Turning to leave, LA MALINCHE blocks his exit.*)

FRIDA

Anything you say to me you can say in front of my alter egos. (*Putting her arms around the other women.*)

DIEGO

Very well. We've been married for thirteen years. I love you too much to cause you further suffering. It's time we parted once and for all.

MALINCHE

(*Mocking him.*) Oh yes, we've heard that before!

FRIDA

Fine! I want an immediate divorce.

DIEGO

That's it? You're not going to put up a fight? Eh, Frida, would a divorce really put an end to it? Wouldn't you suffer even more without me?

FRIDA

Oh, you'll come crawling back, begging me to marry you again.

SOR JUANA

Which, of course, you will decline!

FRIDA

Oh, I might take him back again, but only under certain conditions.

MALINCHE

Don't do it, Frida!

FRIDA

I will provide for myself financially from the proceeds of my art. I will pay half of the household expenses. And I swear, like Lysistrata, we'll have no sexual intercourse!

DIEGO

Do you think I would agree to that?

ALL

Yes!!! (*It is obvious that he has lost. The women celebrate.*)

FRIDA

Good-bye Diego. I'll await your reply! Sor Juana, come! (*Taking SOR JUANA by the arm and walking toward the door.*)

DIEGO

Well, you and Sor Juanita have a "nice" time!

FRIDA

You know, Sor Juana, a man's sex is just in one place, whereas a woman's sexual organs are all over her body!

SOR JUANA

My sentiments exactly. We'll have a lot more fun together! (*They exit merrily on their way, laughing and flirting.*)

DIEGO

(*With a show of bravado.*) Does she really think I care?

MALINCHE

You want her to have affairs with other women just to keep her occupied, don't you!

DIEGO

Of course not, don't be ridiculous!

MALINCHE

You'd rather see her with a woman than with a man!

DIEGO

She's free to do whatever she wants, and so am I! (*He sits down on a table and motions to MALINCHE.*) Bring me a mug of pulque. (*MALINCHE brings it and places it in front of him.*) But why no sex?

MALINCHE

Stupid man, do you think that, with the images of all your other women flashing through her mind, she could possibly make love to you? (*DIEGO thinks about this and nods.*)

DIEGO

You know, when she was just a teenager she told her friends one day, "My ambition is to have a child by Diego Rivera."

MALINCHE

Why would she want to have a child with a potbellied, smelly old goat like you?

DIEGO

Because she said I was tender, wise, and sweet. She said she would bathe me and clean me up so she could have my baby. But then she had the streetcar accident. She was literally impaled on a metal bar in the wreckage. Not only was her spine fractured, but her pelvis was crushed. Thus she suffered miscarriage after miscarriage.

MALINCHE

Frida doesn't need a child.

DIEGO

Why?

MALINCHE

She has you! (*Exit MALINCHE. DIEGO "cries in his beer." The spirit of SOR JUANA appears.*)

SOR JUANA

Stubborn men—so very adept
at wrongly accusing women
not realizing you're to blame
for faults you plant in her mind.
After you've won by urgent plea
the right to tarnish her good name
you still expect her to behave
you, who coaxed her into shame.
You batter her resistance down

and then, with righteousness proclaim
that feminine frivolity
not your stubbornness, is to blame.

*Sound of light rain. Enter a young woman dressed in modish clothes of the late sixties—miniskirt and boots, one with a broken heel. She appears to limp and is scared and tired. She goes to sit down on a nearby bench. Enter JOHNNY dressed like a hippie, long hair, blue jeans, granny glasses, bandana. They look at each other, somewhat startled. She gets up to leave.*

JOHNNY

Don't be afraid. (*As she tries to move away from him, not replying.*) Did you just come from there? Did you see what happened? (*She doesn't reply.*) You're limping. Are you all right? Have a seat.

CARMEN

It's . . . dirty.

JOHNNY

What? The bench? (*He cleans it with a handkerchief.*) There, I cleaned it, sit down. You're going to hurt your foot.

CARMEN

(*Sitting as far away from him as possible. Sounds of sirens. They both tense up.*) What's going on?

JOHNNY

An ambulance passing through. We'll be safe here in the park.

CARMEN

You're not from here, are you?

JOHNNY

No, not exactly. I mean I was born here, but my parents went to live on the other side . . .

CARMEN

In the United States! (*Laughing.*) Then, you're a Pocho!

JOHNNY

(*Somewhat hurt.*) Yeah, I guess that's what you call us, Pochos! Actually, I'm a Chicano.

CARMEN

A Chicano? What's that? (*Before he can answer she blurts out.*) What time is it?

JOHNNY
  Midnight.

CARMEN
  Midnight! My parents are probably worried to death about me.

JOHNNY
  Who are you, Cinderella?

CARMEN
  No, my name is Carmen. You talk funny.

JOHNNY
  I know, I'm trying to learn Spanish. My name is Johnny. You know, all the lights are out in the downtown area.

CARMEN
  Was there a blackout?

JOHNNY
  I don't know . . . I saw some trucks, garbage trucks picking up people!

CARMEN
  What kind of people?

JOHNNY
  Dead people! (*They both stand up at the same time and freeze. Enter DIEGO, who goes and sits on another bench. They are unaware of him.*)

CARMEN
  I have to go call my parents.

JOHNNY
  I wouldn't go out there if I were you. It's dangerous. There was a big demonstration. People took turns making speeches and denouncing the government. I couldn't figure out half of what they said. My Spanish isn't that good. Then all of a sudden they started shooting.

CARMEN
  Who?

JOHNNY
  The soldiers! At the people in the crowd.

CARMEN
  You don't know what you're talking about.

JOHNNY

It just happened! Where have you been?

CARMEN

I was with my friend, Ofelia. She made a date to meet her boyfriend at the cinema to see *The Graduate*, but we never got there. There was a demonstration . . . I don't remember what happened except that we had to leave the car. Oh, the car! My father is going to kill me!

JOHNNY

There was a little boy running next to me. I saw him fall. I looked down, and he didn't have any shoes on. No shoes! (*Sounds of shots being fired in the distance.*) Did you hear that?

CARMEN

I better go home. (*Trying to leave.*)

JOHNNY

It's dangerous out there. Wait a while, we're safe here.

CARMEN

I'm calling the police!

JOHNNY

(*Holding her back.*) You're crazy!

CARMEN

No, you're the one who's crazy, you Pocho! Just look at you, huaraches, long hair, dressed like an Indian. I bet you even smoke marijuana, don't you?

JOHNNY

Well, maybe I do and maybe I don't. But look at you—dressed like a gringa go-go girl. What's so original about that? (*DIEGO laughs, but they cannot see him.*)

CARMEN

What was that? (*Frightened, she sits down next to Johnny.*)

JOHNNY

It was the wind.

CARMEN

For your information, what I am wearing is called "fashion." I've been to London and Paris, and this is what they wear.

JOHNNY

All right, don't get all "uptight."

CARMEN

"Uptight," that's a new word. You're a hippie, aren't you? I've never met a real hippie before. My father says that the American hippies are bringing drugs and venereal diseases into our country.

JOHNNY

Your father must be very intelligent!

CARMEN

Just like the soldiers shooting the people! What are you doing here anyway? Why don't you go back to your own country and do something about Vietnam?

JOHNNY

I have! I marched against the war in Vietnam! I came here to learn how to paint murals.

CARMEN

And smoke marijuana, eat mushrooms, practice free love? Although I don't think they kill people for that. Why would the government do this? What's the reason?

JOHNNY

The Olympic games. The students threatened to demonstrate, but the government didn't want to look weak to the rest of the world.

CARMEN

Killing people because of the games is not logical. It is just as illogical as being here in this stupid park at midnight with a lunatic. I must be having a nightmare!

DIEGO

A nightmare is a place called Tlatelolco! Tlatelolco! (*JOHNNY turns where DIEGO is but sees nothing.*)

CARMEN

(*Scared.*) Did you hear that, someone said "Tlatelolco."

JOHNNY

Yes. But there's no one there.

CARMEN

This is a strange place, I have to get out of here! (*More shots are fired.*)

JOHNNY

Listen, more gunshots. Now do you believe me?

CARMEN

Oh Jesus! Now I remember! We were crossing Reforma Avenue when all of a sudden a mob of people came running toward us. I had to stop the car.

JOHNNY

(*More shots are heard.*) They're still looking for demonstrators. We'd better wait until morning when people come to work and we can hide.

CARMEN

Are you some kind of agitator?

JOHNNY

No, I'm only a student.

CARMEN

This is a horrible city.

JOHNNY

Today it's the most horrible city in the world.

CARMEN

I can't stay here all night. (*She gets up and starts walking, but her ankle hurts too much to walk. He helps her back down again and kneels at her feet, taking off her boot. He examines her ankle with tenderness.*)

JOHNNY

Does it hurt here? (*She lets out a whimper.*) It's swollen . . . you won't be able to walk far on this. It could be sprained. (*He rips open part of his shirt and ties it around her ankle.*) You have feet like Cinderella.

CARMEN

Well, you're not exactly Prince Charming, but you have nice hands. What part of the United States are you from, Johnny?

JOHNNY

Chicago.

CARMEN

Where all the gangsters come from.

JOHNNY

That's a myth. What about you, where do you live?

CARMEN

Lomas de Chapultepec.

JOHNNY

That's where all the rich kids live.

CARMEN

That, Mr. Pocho, is also a myth!

JOHNNY

Stop calling me a Pocho, Carmen. I'm a Chicano, OK? (*Beat.*) I'm going to put your boot on again. If it hurts, let me know.

CARMEN

I'm sorry, Johnny, it's just that after Ofelia and I got separated . . . Ofelia . . . (*Suddenly remembering.*) She's dead! She was shot . . . the windshield shattered . . . she was shot in the head! (*She starts crying.*) She wanted to go to the movie to see her boyfriend. But she didn't have permission from her parents. And now she's dead! (*JOHNNY embraces her, she rests her head on his shoulder.*)

DIEGO

That's better. (*As JOHNNY dries her tears with his handkerchief.*) There are nights when loneliness can only be cured with a kiss.

JOHNNY

Do you mind if I kiss you?

DIEGO

(*As she draws away.*) Insist, my boy, insist!

JOHNNY

Please! (*They kiss. It is short but sweet.*)

CARMEN

You never kissed a Mexican girl before?

JOHNNY

No, only gringas. (*He tries to kiss her again, but she pulls away.*)

CARMEN

Thanks for bandaging my ankle. Look, I saw a phone booth at the entrance to the park. I have to call my father.

JOHNNY

You can't walk. Give me the number. I'll call and tell your father you're at the kiosk in Alameda Park. (*She writes down her number on a piece of paper and gives it to him.*)

CARMEN

Here's my number, with my father's name.

JOHNNY

(*Looking at it in shock.*) Cortés!

CARMEN

Yes, Ramón Cortés. It's a common name. Is something wrong?

JOHNNY

No. Don't go away. I'll be right back.

DIEGO

(*Approaching CARMEN. Now she sees him.*) Young lady, do you know who that young man is?

CARMEN

No, I just met him. Who are you?

DIEGO

I'm Diego Rivera, and that was my assistant. He was going to be your husband.

CARMEN

My husband! What are you talking about?

DIEGO

It was a match made in heaven. It would have reconciled the bad blood between the Indian and the Spanish, the Mexican and Chicano, the North and the South. But the marriage never happened.

CARMEN

I don't understand! I am so confused! (*Realizing the horrible truth.*) Then there was a massacre!

DIEGO

They'll never now how many people really died tonight. Some say thousands.

CARMEN

And you, Diego Rivera?

DIEGO

I'm just reliving this nightmare in my Mexican memory. As for you, a bullet pierced your heart. (*She touches her breast and looks at DIEGO.*)

CARMEN

> Then . . . I'm dead? (*DIEGO nods in the affirmative.*) What about Johnny, is he dead too?

DIEGO

> No, he's alive. He'll go back to Chicago and paint murals on the walls of the city. At this moment your father is telling him that they found your body at the Red Cross. You were lucky to be identified.

CARMEN

> Oh my God! We got caught in the demonstration. We tried to get out but all the streets were cordoned off. The troops started firing! We ran toward the church. They closed the doors! People were crushed against the heavy wooden doors!

DIEGO

> Oh, Carmen, in whose veins runs the blood of Hernán Cortés. Here comes Johnny, in whose veins runs the blood of La Malinche. Even though I can't put you in my mural, because you haven't been born yet, I'll paint you like an Aztec calendar in this scene, in memory of all the young people who died that night in Tlatelolco! (*CARMEN dies. Enter JOHNNY wearing the headdress of an Aztec warrior. He takes her in his arms and holds her like the illustration in a Mexican calendar. Stage picture.*)

*Immediately thereafter the music of Perez Prado is heard. Enter a devil and an angel who dance a macabre mambo of death.*

CHI-CHI

> (*Appearing with a microphone in hand.*) Hello, this is Chi-Chi Batista, reporting live from the Hotel del Prado! The sacrilegious mural *Dreaming on a Sunday in the Alameda* by the atheist artist Diego Rivera has caused a tremendous scandal. University students entered the hotel this morning and defaced portions of it, literally scratching out the face of the blasphemer and Communist painter who wrote the words, "God Does Not Exist!" Imagine that! What an offense! His excellency, the archbishop of Mexico, has righteously refused to bless the newly constructed Hotel del Prado until this profanity is removed. The hotel manager just now covered the mural with a curtain so as not to offend the decent people of the city. And now, back to our regularly scheduled programming . . . (*Fade out.*)

DIEGO

> (*DIEGO enters dressed as a child of twelve in knickers, jacket, and straw hat. There are frogs and snakes in his pockets. He goes directly to his mural and starts painting. FRIDA enters draped in the red flag of the Communist Party. This last scene is filled with haunting music and distorted images as in a dream worthy of Salvador Dali.*) Frida, I'm almost finished with my mural!

FRIDA

> Why are you dressed like that?

DIEGO

> I don't know. This is the outfit I wore when I was twelve and about to enter the Art Academy of San Carlos.

FRIDA

> Could it be that your adolescence has been excessively prolonged? A kind of punishment of the man for stealing years from the boy!

DIEGO

> Look, you're about to observe the crowning touch! (*Sketching "God Does Not Exist."*)

FRIDA

> "God Does Not Exist"!

DIEGO

> But I didn't say it. Ignacio Ramirez said "God Does Not Exist" in an address to the Academy of Letrán, here in the Alameda.

FRIDA

> This mural has already caused a great deal of controversy. The archbishop refuses to bless the hotel, saying it's damned because of your profane work.

DIEGO

> Yes, isn't that lovely? Another cause célèbre!

FRIDA

> Is that why those students are holding a rally down the street?

DIEGO

> Sons of the nouveau riche, Catholics, and Knights of Columbus. All the newspapers are screaming bloody murder! My greatest scandal yet!

FRIDA

> Diego, I came to say good-bye.

DIEGO

What, you're leaving me again?

FRIDA

It's time for me to make my exit from Mexical-Pan-De-Las-Tunas.

DIEGO

Where are you going? Paris? New York? Another art opening? I think you'll become more famous than I one of these days! (*Enter LA CATRINA with a skull mask.*) What an interesting girl, Frida, aren't you going to introduce us?

FRIDA

Diego, this is La Catrina. Catrina, this is Diego. She's all yours! (*Kissing DIEGO.*) Adios, Diego! See you in another life! (*She exits.*)

DIEGO

(*Trying to follow her.*) What are you talking about! Frida! Frida! (*DIEGO clutches his groin in pain.*)

CATRINA

Oh, are you in pain? Let me call someone who can help you! (*Enter SOR JUANA dressed in white like a nurse. LA CATRINA stands off to the side to observe.*)

DIEGO

Nurse! I have this horrible pain, this incredible swelling . . .

SOR JUANA

Where, my boy?

DIEGO

In my pío-pío! I can't take even go pee-pee!

SOR JUANA

(*Clapping her hands.*) Well, you know what that sounds like, my boy. (*Clapping again.*) You have the old . . . (*Clapping again.*)

DIEGO

It's not that. I've had that! It's something much worse.

SOR JUANA

Oh, very well, let's take a look at the poor little overworked member!

DIEGO

(*Shy, like a little boy.*) You!

SOR JUANA

My boy, I'm a nurse. Had men not stood in my way I could have been a world-class physician!

DIEGO

Sorry! (*He reluctantly submits to an examination. Then motioning to the audience.*) But all those people!

SOR JUANA

Never mind them.

DIEGO

(*Sexually aroused.*) Oh Sacred Mother!

SOR JUANA

(*Slapping his hands.*) Señor Rivera, you have a rare case of cancer. I recommend immediate amputation of the penis and testicles to prevent the spread of the malignancy!

DIEGO

No! A thousand times no! I refuse to allow the sacrifice of those organs that have given me the finest pleasure I know. (*SOR JUANA shrugs her shoulders and holds out her hand, demanding a fee, which DIEGO pays. She exits. All at once a chant is heard from offstage.*)

VOICES (*Off*)

Does He exist?

Long live Jesus Christ!

Death to Diego Rivera!

CORTÉS

(*Entering with a jar of paint.*) Are you going to erase the words "God Does Not Exist"?

DIEGO

Of course not, I stand by everything. It's the historical truth!

CORTÉS

Very well then! (*Throwing paint on DIEGO's mural.*) Take that!

DIEGO

(*Going after him.*) You barbarian! Deface my mural! That's an act of cultural vandalism! (*They scuffle.*)

CORTÉS

I've had enough of your impudence! (*Taking out his sword. DIEGO pulls out a long paintbrush and playfully duels with CORTÉS.*

*CORTÉS, however, is deadly serious and stabs DIEGO repeatedly. DIEGO falls. Then, to the audience.*) The fatherland or death! White Warriors Union! (*He exits.*)

CATRINA

Oh, my child, my poor child, are you hurt?

DIEGO

Stop him! Did you see what he did?

CATRINA

It's all right, Diego, it's only a dream. Close your eyes.

DIEGO

What am I dreaming of, Catrina?

CATRINA

Your life, your work.

DIEGO

What was Johnny dreaming?

CATRINA

Of Mexican culture in the North.

DIEGO

And Sor Juana?

CATRINA

Of being born in a different time!

DIEGO

Of course! And Frida was dreaming of me and of her painting. And La Malinche of being in my mural. My mural! What have they done to my mural? There was an earthquake and they moved it somewhere.

CATRINA

Don't worry, we're painted here forever. No one will ever erase us! (*Embracing him.*) Will you be my mine? Will you sleep with me? Forever?

DIEGO

Yes, Catrina my calaca flaca, let us lie together. Let us bind our bones together. Imagine the noise when we fuck!

CATRINA

Deep in the bowels of the earth. Don't be afraid, my little one. (*She unbuttons her blouse and offers him a bony teat.*)

DIEGO

What marvelous breasts you have!

CATRINA

The better to devour me like a fruit.

DIEGO

I'm so hungry!

CATRINA

Drink, drink, drink your fill!

DIEGO

(*Trying to devour her.*) So juicy, so tender, so succulent!

CATRINA

(*DIEGO reaches a climax.*) There, there my little one.

DIEGO

Catrina, what are you dreaming of?

CATRINA

Of you Diego, of you. All of us are dreaming of you!

*All the players enter and get in place as if in the actual mural. HERNÁN CORTÉS with his bloody hands, FRIDA holding her sphere symbolizing yin and yang, SOR JUANA in her nun's habit, DON PORFIRIO in his majestic uniform, DIEGO holding LA CATRINA's hand. The music swells. Slow fade.*

## The End

# Esperanza

## An Opera in Two Acts

Adapted from the screenplay by Michael Wilson
Libretto by Carlos Morton
Additional lyrics by David Bishop
Music by David Bishop

# Characters*

RAMÓN QUINTERO: a Mexican American miner
ESPERANZA QUINTERO: Ramón's wife
ESTELA: Ramón and Esperanza's ten-year-old daughter
VICENTE VIDAL: a miner, Ramón's compadre
TERESA VIDAL: Vicente's wife, Esperanza's comadre
MRS. SALAZAR: a miner's widow
SALVADOR RUIZ: a miner; also SHERIFF'S DEPUTY
FRANK BARNES: union organizer, Anglo
SUPERINTENDENT ALEXANDER, Anglo
CHIEF FOREMAN BARTON, Anglo; also SHERIFF
JESUSITA, LOLA, ADELITA: Miners' wives
Also assorted miners and sheriff's deputies

*The opera can be performed by eight women and six men.

# The Scene

*In and around Zinc Town, southern New Mexico. The landscape is dominated by the Delaware Zinc's mine, with its shaft, conveyor belt, and mountain of tailings. Close by lies the miners' shantytown, including the Quintero family cottage with its yard and interior living space. Other playing areas include the union hall, a beer parlor, and a jail. The apron can be used as a neutral space where the miners picket, and simultaneous actions can occur on other parts of the stage. The staging should be "nonrealistic"—steel bars that fly down to represent the jail, a counter with stools for the bar, and benches for the union hall.*

# Time

*Early 1950s.*

# Act 1

*Afternoon. Outside a row of shanties occupied by the Mexican miners of Zinc Town and their families, the women are washing clothes, boiling water, and chopping wood.)*

WOMEN
   Chop wood for breakfast, chop wood for clothes,
   Chop wood to heat the stove. Heat the iron,
   Cook breakfast, send the kids off to school.

JESUSITA
   (*Holding up a pair of pants.*) How am I ever going to get these pants clean?

TERESA
   The zinc from the mine never comes out.

LOLA
   Mrs. Sanderson is looking for a maid. Anybody interested?

MRS. SALAZAR
   Part-time or live-in?

WOMEN
   Sweep the house, scrub the floors,
   Chop wood for dinner, cook their dinner,
   Wash the dishes.

TERESA

And you know what he says
When he gets home:
"What ya been doing all day woman,
Reading the funny papers?"

MRS. SALAZAR

I went to the company store, and they refuse to give me credit anymore!

JESUSITA

That's not right, that's not fair, you're a widow!

*Enter ESTELA on her way home from school.*

ESTELA

Riqui-ran, riqui-ran, los Maderos de San Juan,
Piden pan, no les dan, piden queso, les dan un hueso,
¡Y se les atora en el pescuezo!

WOMEN

(*Simultaneously with ESTELA.*)
Chop wood for breakfast, chop wood for clothes,
Chop wood to heat the stove. Heat the iron, cook the breakfast,
Send the kids off to school.

MRS. SALAZAR

(*To ESTELA.*) Here Estelita, these are the flowers I promised your mother.

ESTELA

(*Simultaneous with above.*)
Ricki-ran, ricki-ran, the woodcutters from San Juan,
Ask for bread, they get a stone.

MRS. SALAZAR

Ask for cheese they get a bone, and it sticks in their throat. (*Beat.*) Estela, aren't you supposed to be in school?

ESTELA

Yes, Mrs. Salazar, I'm on my way. ¡Adiós!

*Enter BARTON, the foremen, and ALEXANDER, the superintendent. BARTON is dressed in overalls, while ALEXANDER sports a suit and Stetson hat.*

BARTON

This here's the "Meskin" part of town. First time in New Mexico, Mr. Alexander?

ALEXANDER

(*With a handkerchief.*) Yes, I live back east, near company head-quarters. Barton, what's that god-awful smell?

BARTON

Running sewers. That's the way these people live. You'll get used to it. (*They exit.*)

ESTELA

(*Goes to her mother as ESPERANZA emerges from the interior of her house. Gives her the flowers.*)
Mami, are you sick?

ESPERANZA

No, Estelita. (*Smelling the flowers.*) ¡Qué flores tan bonitas!

ESTELA

Mami, are you sad?

ESPERANZA

Just tired, Estelita, muy cansada.

ESTELA

Are we going to church, are we going to Mass?

ESPERANZA

After I finish the ironing.

ESTELA

It's your birthday, it's your Saint's Day.

ESPERANZA

After I cook our dinner.

ESTELA

Mami, don't worry, after the baby comes,
I'll help you cook, I'll help you iron,
Help you chop wood, wash clothes,
Watch the baby.

ESPERANZA

No, Estelita, I don't want you doing this,
Day after day, the same monotony.
Estela, it's late! Why aren't you in school?

ESTELA

 I don't want to go to school.

ESPERANZA

 Why not? Tell me.

ESTELA

 Miss Johnson's mean! Says we don't know how to speak good
 English.
 Calls us names, says we're lazy, stupid!

ESPERANZA

 You go to school, Estela, right now, go to school and tell that teacher
 you're not lazy.
 Tell her you're not stupid.

ESTELA

 Yes, Mami.

ESPERANZA

 I'll go myself, later, and have a word with Miss Johnson.
 (*ESTELA gets her books and leaves.*)
 How many times has this happened?
 What kind of teachers are they?
 That's not the way to teach a child,
 Telling her she's lazy, stupid!
 Don't they know she didn't speak English until she was five?
 She's ten now. It took her longer, but now she speaks two languages,
 one more than they!
 I never got much schooling, Estela has to go to high school, maybe
 even college.
 Marry someone worthy, a lawyer or a doctor. Or perhaps a miner
 like her father.

(*Lights up slowly on the other side of the stage, revealing RAMÓN crawling
around in a mine shaft, the light from his helmet illuminating his
surroundings.*)
 I don't really care, I just want her to have a better life.
 Miner, doctor, lawyer, farmer, as long as he's an honest man, as long
 as he's a worthy man.
 As long as he's a kind man like her father, someone she can respect
 and stand next to.
 As equals side by side, as equals side by side.

(*The music intensifies as RAMÓN lights a fuse and runs away. Explosion. She runs toward the mine, but RAMÓN and FRANK meet her halfway, walking out of a cloud of dust.*)

Ramón, my God, what happened?

FRANK

There was an accident! I told the company we need two men working with the dynamite.

RAMÓN

The force of the blast threw me on the floor.

ESPERANZA

Your clothes are torn!

RAMÓN

This is the last straw! The dynamite. It almost blew up in my face!

FRANK

And as your union rep, I am going to file a grievance, I promise you that!

ESPERANZA

(*ESPERANZA takes RAMÓN and sits him down.*) You go on ahead, Frank, I'll take care of him. (*Exit FRANK.*) Ramón, this job is too dangerous. Maybe you should quit. We could move to Albuquerque or El Paso.

RAMÓN

No Esperanza, we can't give up now.

ESPERANZA

I don't want anything to happen to you!

RAMÓN

Don't worry, querida, I'll be all right. (*Trying to wash up.*) This water's cold again.

ESPERANZA

I'm sorry, the fire's gone out. (*She begins to stoke the stove.*)

RAMÓN

Forget it.

ESPERANZA

I chop wood for the fire five times a day. But the Anglo miners on the other side of the tracks have hot water and bathrooms in their homes.

RAMÓN

Do you think I like living this way?

ESPERANZA

Can't the union get us decent plumbing?

RAMÓN

It was one of the demands.

ESPERANZA

Was?

RAMÓN

We had to drop it. Right now safety is the most important issue. Five accidents this year, all because of speedup. You're a woman, you don't know what it's like down there!

ESPERANZA

I see, you'll strike for your demands. But if we wives want something, that comes later.

RAMÓN

Is that all you care about, your own comfort? Can't you think of anyone except yourself?

ESPERANZA

It's not just me, it's the children, it's all of us!

RAMÓN

I have to go talk to the men in the union. (*He starts to leave.*)

ESPERANZA

Ramón, wait! I have something to say! (*He exits, leaving ESPERANZA alone with her thoughts.*)
What kind of world am I bringing this child into?
No hot water, running sewers,
Ramón and I arguing constantly,
The teacher insulting Estela.
I wish this child I am carrying might never be born!
No, not in this world, not in this world.
(*Exit ESPERANZA.*)

*The cantina. Enter RAMÓN as the other men greet him. MRS. SALAZAR is behind the bar.*

RAMÓN

Hola brothers!

MEN

Hola Ramón!

RAMÓN

I've had it, we can't go on living this way.

MEN

Can't go on living this way!

VICENTE

I didn't fight in World War II to come home to this.

SALVADOR

To come home to this!

VICENTE

I say we go on strike, close down the mine!

MEN

Close it down, close down the mine!

SALVADOR

But if we do that, who'll pay the bills? Who'll pay the rent? Feed our families? (*Motioning to MRS. SALAZAR, who brings him another beer and serves it.*) Señora, give the boys a round on me.

MRS. SALAZAR

Put it on your tab? (*SALVADOR nods in the affirmative, as she goes behind the counter to tally up and serve the beers.*)
Oh, the bills on the bar soak up too much beer by far,
And they say, time to pay, time you headed for home.
Oh, the bills you collect when your senses are wrecked,
Will I fear, cost you dear, time you headed for home.

SALVADOR

You don't strike when the bosses want, you wait for the right time, that's how you win.

RAMÓN

Does the company doctor wait? "That'll be twenty bucks."
Does the company store wait? "Pay or we take it away."
Well, I don't like it. I'm fed up. We can't wait.

MEN

I don't like it. I'm fed up. We can't wait.

FRANK

If you go on strike, the men in the other unions will help out.

SALVADOR

Too many debts, too many bills to pay. And you, Ramón, with another kid on the way.

FRANK

You almost got killed out there.

RAMÓN

Safety is the first demand.

MEN

Safety is the first demand!

VICENTE

And them damn Anglos, excuse me Frank, present company excluded, make twice as much as we do!

MEN

Equal pay for equal work!

MRS. SALAZAR

Don't forget the sanitation issue! (*The miners ignore her.*)

FRANK

An eight-hour day, and extra pay for overtime!

MEN

Eight-hour day and extra pay!

MRS. SALAZAR

How about hot water, toilets, sewers!

RAMÓN

(*To MRS. SALAZAR.*) Yeah sure, we'll get to that, but first things first!

VICENTE

Mrs. Salazar, how about another round?

RAMÓN

(*Drinking the rest of his beer.*) I'm ready.

VICENTE

Frank?

FRANK

I'll have one too.

MRS. SALAZAR

(*Writing up different tabs for different men. And passing them along.*)
Well, Salvador that's ten, Vicente six for you, Ramón three, Frank
two.

MEN

Oh, the bills on the bar soak up too much beer by far,
And they say, time to pay, time we headed for home.

MRS. SALAZAR

(*To RAMÓN.*) Ramón, what are you doing here? Don't you realize
what day it is?

RAMÓN

Thursday?

MRS. SALAZAR

It's Esperanza's Saint's Day.

RAMÓN

¡Qué tonto! (*To the other men.*) Hey boys, how about getting me out
of the doghouse by going back and singing "Las Mañanitas" to mi
esposa? (*They all agree it's time to go.*)

MEN

Oh, the bills on the bar soak up too much beer by far,
And they say, time to pay, time we headed for home.

MRS. SALAZAR

Yes the bills you collect when your senses are wrecked,
Will I fear cost you dear, time you headed for home.

*The men exit the cantina, lighting their way with flashlights and lanterns.*
*They are joined by the women. Singing as they walk, a procession that grows*
*in intensity over to the Quintero household. Lights up in ESPERANZA's*
*room.*

CHORUS

Estas son Las Mañanitas
que cantaba el Rey David,
A las muchachas bonitas
te las cantamos a ti.
Despierta, mi bien, despierta,

mira que ya amaneció,
Ya los pajaritos cantan,
la luna ya se metió.

ESTELA

(*As the group approaches the house, ESTELA opens the door, and the musicians take their places.*) Mami, Papi didn't forget! He's come to sing you "Las Mañanitas"! (*Bringing the cake.*) Can we light the candles on the cake now?

ESPERANZA

Yes, we can light the candles. (*MRS. SALAZAR helps ESTELA light the candles.*)

ALL

El día en que tu naciste,
nacieron todas las flores.
En la pila del bautismo,
cantaron los ruiseñores,
Ya viene amaneciendo,
ya la luz del día nos vio,
¡Levántate, Esperanza,
mira que ya amaneció!

*The song ends in laughter and applause. ESPERANZA blows out the candles. Bottles of beer are passed around, and the party begins. RAMÓN is the last to enter.*

RAMÓN

(*To ESPERANZA, they are alone, yet surrounded by family and friends.*) Why are you crying?

ESPERANZA

For a lot of reasons. You shouldn't have gone to so much trouble. It must have been expensive.

RAMÓN

The boys chipped in for beer, and the ladies brought the food.

ESPERANZA

I thought you had forgotten, you have a lot on your mind!

RAMÓN

I have to confess, I did forget! Mrs. Salazar reminded me it was your Saint's Day.

ESPERANZA

(*Kissing him.*) You've always been an honest man, of that I am very grateful. (*They stand together in an embrace, listening to the music.*)

RAMÓN

Dance with me.

ESPERANZA

(*Playful.*) No, I can't.

RAMÓN

Come on, dance with me.

ESPERANZA

I am not allowed.

RAMÓN

Who won't allow it?

ESPERANZA

Our child! (*RAMÓN is puzzled, ESPERANZA takes his hand and places it on her stomach.*) Here, do you feel him move?
The baby wants to tell you he's here listening to us.
(*Holding RAMÓN's hand to her stomach.*)
Bebé, this is your father, he wants to talk to you.
His voice is the voice, so weary after work, often grumpy.
He calls for his supper, says "the water is cold."
Can you hear that? Don't pay any attention!
All day the ground trembles as he blasts the ore
From the bowels of the earth.
All day in the mine shaft, breathing dust and danger.
Working with his compadres.
Can you hear that? Can you hear as he shouts orders?
Can you hear the men respond?
In their voices can you hear the confidence that he inspires?
Can you hear your sister's laughter as he holds her in his arms?
Can you hear his love for us, for you?
We have little time to laugh, or time to play.
Just time for tears. When you come into this world
Your father will welcome you.
When you come into this world your father will cherish you.
Can you hear that?

RAMÓN

> Hello, little one. Still hiding in your mother's womb?
> Boy or girl? I don't care.
> Today is your mother's Saint's Day. Don't you want to come out?
> Don't you want to come out and celebrate with us?
> Your mother can't dance while you are still inside her.
> Too bad, because she's a good dancer
> Although we don't have much time for dancing anymore.
> But we'll have time to celebrate your birthday
> The day you're born.

ESPERANZA/RAMÓN

> So for now, so for now,
> Dance for us, since we cannot.
> Dance for us, stretch out your arms and legs
> Spinning like a top, doing somersaults.
> Practice dancing, laughing, playful child of ours.
> We wait for you, we welcome you, we live for you.

*The next morning. The people of Zinc Town are already up and about, the women tending to their chores, the men working at the mine. ESTELA is in the kitchen with her mother, playing a game as they heat up a batch of hot chocolate in a pot.*

ESTELA

> Uno, dos, tres, BA
> Uno, dos, tres, TE.

ESPERANZA

> Uno, dos, tres, CHO.
> Uno, dos, tres, CO.

ESTELA/ESPERANZA

> Uno, dos, tres, LA.
> Uno, dos, tres, TE.
> (*Whipping up the chocolate with a wooden mallet.*)
> Ba-te, ba-te, el cho-co-late!
> (*ESPERANZA and ESTELA laugh but are interrupted by three sharp blasts of a whistle.*)

VARIOUS WOMEN

> Accident! (*Running toward the mine, women and children.*)
> ¡Accidente!

MRS. SALAZAR

    ¡Dios mío! ¿Qué pasó?

VICENTE

    Kalinsky broke his leg!

*In front of the mine, we see an injured man lying on the ground. Two miners lift him up on a stretcher and carry him offstage. A woman follows them offstage, crying. Enter superintendent ALEXANDER with foreman BARTON. They square off and face RAMÓN and the other miners.*

ALEXANDER

    How did it happen?

BARTON

    Kalinsky wandered into a drift, while this fellow (*Indicating RAMÓN.*) was blasting.

RAMÓN

    (*Dirty, sweating, furious, yelling at BARTON.*)
    There, you see, I told you, it takes two men to do that!
    That man's lucky to be alive, he could have gotten killed!

BARTON

    Look here, Pancho, I checked the shaft just before the blast.
    You didn't shout the warning!

RAMÓN

    You weren't even there, you were sitting in the office drinking coffee!

BARTON

    You're a liar!

RAMÓN

    Drinking coffee.

BARTON

    You're a liar!

RAMÓN

    In the office drinking coffee!

BARTON

    No-good dirty spic! (*RAMÓN rushes at him and they fight. The miners pull them apart.*) You don't like it here, go back where you came from!

RAMÓN

Eighteen years I have worked in this mine, eighteen years of dynamite and darkness.

Go back where I came from? This is my home, San Marcos, Zinc Town.

Where would you have me go? What would you have me do?

Before the Anglos came, my great-grandfather raised cattle on this plain.

Before the Anglos came, my grandfather owned this land where the mine stands.

Now it belongs to the company.

Before the Anglos came, our roots grew deep in this soil,

Deeper than the pinos, deeper than the mine shaft.

Can you pull up the pines by their roots and say, "Go back where you came from"?

Can you blast the ore from the soil and say, "Go somewhere else"?

This is where I come from. This is my home!

ALEXANDER

You there, get a hold of yourself!

I know a man's been hurt, but I'm just as sorry as you are, savvy?

Accidents are costly for everyone, especially for the company.

But now let's say we all get back to work, savvy?

*The miners are immobile, no one moves.*

BARTON

All right, fellows, no reason to treat this like a paid holiday. Get back to work!

RAMÓN

¿Ahora sí?

VICENTE

¡Creo que sí!

ALEXANDER

What are they saying?

FRANK

No saaaaaavvy.

ALEXANDER

Damn it, Barnes, you're the union rep, tell them to get back to work!

FRANK

They don't work for me, I work for them.

ALEXANDER

All right, get back to work! Or I'll fire the lot of you!

RAMÓN

(*To the other miners.*) What do you say? (*There is little hesitation. One by one the men vote with a nod of their heads or a simple "sí."*) ¡Chente, apágalo! (*The mine is shut down.*)

BARTON

Get back to work, back to work!

MINERS

¡Huelga! ¡Huelga! We're on strike!

ALEXANDER

You're all fired! Did you hear me, fired! (*The men stand their ground. Exit BARTON and ALEXANDER, furious.*)

MINERS

¡Huelga! ¡Huelga! We're on strike!

*Later that afternoon. Enter ESPERANZA, TERESA, LOLA, JESUSITA, and MRS. SALAZAR.*

TERESA

How can we get these canijos, obstinate men, thoughtless men,
Guys who forget they have wives who work as hard as they do.

WOMEN

Harder, harder, hard as they do. Harder, harder.

TERESA

How can we get these canijos
To put plumbing and sanitation back on the list of demands?

MRS. SALAZAR

Don't forget medical care.

LOLA

I don't know, maybe we should just let the men handle this.

JESUSITA

It's the squeaky wheel that gets the attention, Lola.

WOMEN

Lola, we want plumbing and sanitation, hot water and medical care.
Lola, if we don't raise our voices they won't hear.
It's the squeaky wheel that gets the attention.
They won't hear unless we speak, we can't stand
For lack of your comprehension.
Give us our plumbing and sanitation.
If we don't let them know where we stand, Lola,
We'll keep living like people in caves, Lola,
And they probably won't give a damn, Lola.
We want our say!

*Enter the men.*

RAMÓN

Afternoon, ladies!

LOLA

Buenas tardes.

MRS. SALAZAR

We came to help out.

RAMÓN

We could use some coffee, it's going to get cold tonight.

TERESA

That wasn't what we had in mind.

MRS. SALAZAR

I'll brew up a pot. (*She goes to fill a pot of water.*)

TERESA

(*Pointing to a picket sign.*) That's not how you spell "picket," it only
has one "t."

VICENTE

All right, here, you do it. I can't spell in English. (*Handing TERESA
and the other women the picket signs.*) Oye, where's Salvador Ruiz?

FRANK

Ain't seen him all day. (*Some of the miners exit.*)

*Enter ALEXANDER and the SHERIFF dressed in his uniform. They are
unnoticed by the miners, who have started to picket.*

SHERIFF

So, Mr. Alexander, what'll I charge 'em with? Trespassing on private property?

ALEXANDER

Well, it's all company property, the mine, the store, the shantytown.

SHERIFF

What happened to those new fellows you hired from out of town?

ALEXANDER

They saw how big that picket line was growing and wanted no part it.

SHERIFF

They don't look so tough to me. What if I bash a few heads in?

ALEXANDER

No, there's more than one way to skin a cat.

*RAMÓN spots ALEXANDER and walks over to him as the picketing continues in the background. Deputy Vance stands off to the side.*

RAMÓN

Mr. Alexander! You ready to negotiate? This strike ain't good for business.

ALEXANDER

And it doesn't put tortillas and frijoles on your table.

RAMÓN

Then settle! Our demands are reasonable.

ALEXANDER

Look here, hombre, I saw your work record, it's excellent!
You know you were in line for foreman before this trouble started?
You had a real future with this company, but you let those Reds stir you up.
And now they'll sell you down the river. Why don't you wake up, Ray?
It's your nombre, isn't it, Ray?

RAMÓN

My name is Quintero—Mister Quintero to you! And we are not "Reds," we're red-blooded Americans.

ALEXANDER

Very well, Kin-Tear-Roo, have it your way! (*Turns on his heel and exits in a huff.*)

RAMÓN

(*Turning back to the other miners.*) Hey, guess what? They wanted to make *me* foreman! Can you imagine! What a line! (*The men laugh and slap RAMÓN on the back.*)
De Texas a California,
La gente está cantando.

CHORUS

From Texas to California,
All the people come to sing.
El picket sign, el picket sign!
We carry it all the time!

RAMÓN

De Fresno a San Antonio,
La raza está llamando.

CHORUS

From Fresno to San Antonio
All the people are calling out.
El picket line, el picket line
We're marching all the time!

FRANK

(*Running in, out of breath*) We just saw two scabs in the arroyo!

VICENTE

Let's go get 'em!

RAMÓN

Hold it! Vicente, you come with me. The rest of you stay on the line! (*Exit RAMÓN and VICENTE. Some of the men continue picketing, while the women take up the chant. MRS. SALAZAR picks up a picket sign and joins the line for the first time.*)

CHORUS

El picket sign, el picket sign!
We carry it all the time!

(*Off to the side we see that VICENTE has cornered a scab. RAMÓN is stunned to discover it is SALVADOR RUIZ.*)

RAMÓN

   ¡Salvador! ¡Qué chingaos estás haciendo!

SALVADOR

   Ramón, I'm in a jam, you know, my abuelita is in the hospital.

RAMÓN

   Desgraciado, don't you think we all have problems?

SALVADOR

   I know I did wrong, just let me go, I promise to leave town.

RAMÓN

   Did you think I was going to work you over? I wouldn't dirty my hands with you! (*RAMÓN spits in SALVADOR's face and shoves him. SALVADOR falls hard to the ground. Enter the SHERIFF, who grabs RAMÓN, twisting his arms behind his back and handcuffing him.*)

RAMÓN

   What are you arresting me for? I didn't do nothing.

SHERIFF

   You're under arrest for assault and battery. I saw you slug this man.

RAMÓN

   That's a lie. I didn't . . .

SHERIFF

   (*Slapping RAMÓN across the face with a gloved hand.*) You know that ain't no way to talk to a white man. (*He shoves RAMÓN. They exit.*)

*Simultaneously, on the picket line we see LOLA, MRS. SALAZAR, and ESPERANZA. ESPERANZA cries out and doubles over in pain, as though from a severe cramp.*

LOLA

   ¡Dios mío, Dios mío! (*Immobilized, standing helplessly.*) Mrs. Salazar, come quickly!

MRS. SALAZAR

   Don't just stand there, she's going to have her baby! Help me carry her over to the shack. (*LOLA and MRS. SALAZAR carry ESPERANZA into the shack.*)

ESPERANZA

   God forgive me, wishing this child would never be born. (*Crying out in pain.*).

VICENTE

(*Running over to the jail.*) Ramón, your wife is having the baby!

RAMÓN

(*Struggling with the SHERIFF.*) Let me go, let me go! I have to be with her!

SHERIFF

Sorry, amigo! You're going to jail! (*RAMÓN tries to break away, but the SHERIFF detains him and pulls out his billy club.*) Resisting arrest are you! (*Beating RAMÓN as they exit.*)

VICENTE

(*Following them offstage.*) Hey! You don't have to beat him like that!

MRS. SALAZAR

(*Focus back at the shack.*) Gently! Now, push, push, push!

ESPERANZA

Where is my Ramón, where is my husband? (*The sound of a baby crying.*)

LOLA

It's a boy Esperanza! A healthy baby boy!

ESPERANZA

(*Holding her baby.*) I want him to see our son, our Juanito.
Poor baby, born in a shack, your father in jail.

RAMÓN

(*We see RAMÓN behind bars, bruised and beaten.*)
My son, Juanito Quintero.
Born in a shack, his father in jail.
What kind of life can I give you?

MRS. SALAZAR

(*With supreme irony.*) New Mexico!

RAMÓN

The son of a man who works in a mine,
Will you have to follow my path there?

MRS. SALAZAR

New Mexico, the Land of Enchantment, enchanting for tourists, they flock to its vistas.
New Mexico, the Land of Enchantment, come photograph Natives Dressed up so quaintly, New Mexico.
Serapes and burros, kachina dolls, cactus and Native pottery.

CHORUS

> Born in a shack, your father in jail, what kind of life can he give you?
> Juanito Quintero.
> The son of a man who works in a mine,
> Will you have to follow his path there?
> Juanito Quintero.

RAMÓN

> You will learn, Juanito, we will teach you the ways,
> The ways of our people, Juanito.
> A proud race we were, a proud race we are,
> In the land of our forefathers,
> Who came north from Mexico,
> To found and settle Nuevo México, the New Mexico!

CHORUS

> The Land of Enchantment, enchanting for tourists, they flock to its vistas, New Mexico!
> The Land of Enchantment, come photograph Natives, dressed up so quaintly, New Mexico!
> Nuevo México! The New Mexico!

(*Lights out on the above. Enter the SHERIFF and ALEXANDER from another part of the stage.*)

SHERIFF

> I had to release Quintero, his thirty days are up. But I think we got 'em on the run.

ALEXANDER

> Not quite. These people are as hard as this rock scrabble dirt.
> Been here too long, takes more than that to blow them away.

SHERIFF

> What then?

ALEXANDER

> The final indignity. An injunction cooked up by Taft and Hartley prohibiting them from picketing.

SHERIFF

> And if they disobey?

ALEXANDER

> Jail sentences for the strikers, heavy fines they'll pay. (*They exit.*)

*The people pour into the union hall.*

JESUSITA

Can they really arrest all the miners?

FRANK

They'd like nothing better!

RAMÓN

It's just a trick to break the strike.

VICENTE

What will this injunction do?

TERESA

Keep you from picketing. But only the men! Think about it!

MRS. SALAZAR

I'd like to meet this Taft Hartley guy and tell him a thing or two!

RAMÓN

Quiet everybody! Let's hear what our union rep has to say!

FRANK

If we obey the court, the scabs will move in and the strike will be lost.
If we defy the court, the pickets will be arrested and the strike will be lost.

LOLA

They got us coming and going, we're done for either way.

FRANK

No matter what you decide, the International will back you up. It's your decision!

RAMÓN

If we give up now, we give up fifty years of struggle. I say we defy the injunction!

VICENTE

How? They'll arrest us. We'll gain nothing!

TERESA

Brother Chairmen!

VICENTE

Order! Order!

TERESA

> Read the court injunction carefully.
> It only prohibits "striking miners" from picketing.
> We women are not striking miners.
> We'll take over your picket line. (*A few jeers, raucous male laughter.*)

JESUSITA

> Don't laugh! We have a solution. You have none.
> If we take your places on the picket line the strike will not be broken,
> And no scabs will take your jobs.

RAMÓN

> Let our women do this, and we'll be the laughing stock of the labor movement!

TERESA

> What's worse? To hide behind a woman's skirt or get down on your knees before the boss?

VICENTE

> If our own women can't help us, who can?

RAMÓN

> Women on the picket line, it's a ridiculous idea!

LOLA

> He's right, picketing ain't proper, ladylike. The priest said it might even be a sin!

JESUSITA

> Sit down, Lola!

RAMÓN

> Fellow union members, I say we take a vote!

TERESA

> No fair! You men get to vote on something that affects all of us, men and women.

MRS. SALAZAR

> My husband died in that mine fighting for our rights.

VICENTE

> Mrs. Salazar has a point. I say we adjourn the union meeting and call a community meeting. That way everyone can vote.

RAMÓN
Are you nuts?

VICENTE
All those in favor of adjourning the union meeting say "Aye."

CHORUS
(*Strong response.*) Aye!

VICENTE
Opposed?

RAMÓN
No!

VICENTE
The "Ayes" have it. This union meeting is dissolved, and the community meeting is called to order. Mrs. Salazar, would you like to make a motion?

MRS. SALAZAR
I move that we take a vote to let us women take over the picket line.

TERESA
I second the motion.

VICENTE
All those in favor? Let's have a show of hands! (*ESPERANZA raises her hand defiantly. RAMÓN is furious.*) All those opposed? (*Fewer hands go up, RAMÓN's being one of them.*) The motion has been carried! (*The women celebrate. RAMÓN stands off to the side, sulking.*)

WOMEN
We march, las mujeres today,
Rise before dawn,
And march on.

(*The men hand over the picket signs as the women start to form a line. ESPERANZA goes over to RAMÓN.*)

ESPERANZA
Ramón, all the women are going. It's not fair, I should be there.

RAMÓN
No you're not, and that's that.

ESPERANZA
But the motion passed!

RAMÓN

> The union doesn't run my house.

ESPERANZA

> Can't I even put in an appearance?

RAMÓN

> With a baby in your arms!

ESPERANZA

> The baby likes to be walked, it helps him burp.

MRS. SALAZAR

> (*Signaling her to join the line.*) ¡Esperanza! ¡Ven con nosotros!

ESPERANZA

> I have to be there! (*ESPERANZA runs off to join the picket line before RAMÓN can stop her.*)

RAMÓN

> Esperanza! Get back here right now.

MEN

> Did we do the right thing? I hope we won't be sorry!
> But if there's going to be a fight, you bet the cops will worry.

WOMEN

> We march, las mujeres, today.
> A thousand strong,
> And we'll keep marching on.

ESPERANZA

> By sun up we formed the picket line,
> Women we had never seen before, each carrying a picket sign.

MEN

> There's my tía Guadalupe, and my cousin Jesusita.
> Grandmamas, nietas, and the fiery Adelita.

CHORUS

> A long snaking line from the mountain
> Marched down.
> And there at the mine a cause,
> A common cause we found.
> Daughters, wives, abuelas, we stood our ground.

# End Act 1

## Act 2

*Early morning in Zinc Town. The stage is split into two groups. On one side the women are setting up the picket line. We see ESPERANZA with the baby in her arms, TERESA, MRS. SALAZAR, and others, warming themselves over a campfire. In front of the Quintero cottage, RAMÓN and VICENTE are hanging out the wash.*

VICENTE
(*From the other side of the fence.*) ¿Cómo van las cosas?

RAMÓN
Lousy! No thanks to you, 'Chente.

VICENTE
Come on, Ramón, I was just trying to be fair.

RAMÓN
Letting those women take over the meeting. Now look at us!
Nunca se acaba, it never ends! Three hours! Just to heat enough water and wash these clothes.

VICENTE
Te digo una cosa, I ain't going back to work unless the company installs hot running water for us. Should have been a demand from the very beginning.

RAMÓN
(*Grudgingly.*) Yeah, I guess so! (*They go back to hanging up the clothes.*) What I wouldn't give to have some hot running water.

RAMÓN/VICENTE
Hot running water! Hot running water!

*The focus shifts to the picket line. The women are drinking coffee except for ESPERANZA, who is feeding the baby with a bottle. ESTELA plays nearby.*

ESPERANZA
I usually keep Juanito in the coffee shack.
But when the weather is good and there is peace on the line,
I bring the crib outside.

TERESA
Why doesn't Ramón watch the baby?

ESPERANZA

It's hard enough getting him to do the housework. The other day we had an argument.

RAMÓN

(*The focus shifts to the other side of the stage as RAMÓN talks to VICENTE.*) If you think I'm going to play nursemaid, you're crazy! I've had these kids all day!

ESPERANZA

(*To TERESA.*) And I had them since the day they were born.

RAMÓN

I tell you, I ain't staying home with the baby no more!

ESPERANZA

Then, tomorrow I'll take him with me to the picket line! And I did.

TERESA/VICENTE

That's telling 'em! Stick up for your rights!

*Enter ALEXANDER, the SHERIFF, and a DEPUTY.*

ESPERANZA

Uh-oh, we got company!

DEPUTY

Hello, girls, would you like to see my pistol?

ALEXANDER

Stop joking around and arrest them. Can't you see they're flaunting a court order?

SHERIFF

Don't get excited, they'll scatter like a covey of quail.

ALEXANDER

Let's get at it—before another hundred dames show up.

SHERIFF

All right, boys! (*Pulling out his billy club.*) Let's do it! (*The SHERIFF and his DEPUTY walk toward the line, billy clubs in hand. The women stop marching and turn in unison to face them.*)

RAMÓN

(*Hearing shouts coming from the picket line.*) Come on, let's go!

*The DEPUTY knocks down TERESA, who falls hard on the ground. Other women rush to her side. The SHERIFF and DEPUTY try to use their billy clubs, but there are two women to each man, and the women hold their ground.*

ESPERANZA

    (*As RAMÓN enters, she hands him the baby.*)
    Get back! Get back! Stay out of this! They'll arrest you!

RAMÓN

    (*To VICENTE.*) Don't just stand there! Do something!

*ESPERANZA and TERESA join forces to knock down the DEPUTY.*

VICENTE

    Look's like they're doing fine! (*Pointing to the baby.*) Besides, you got your hands full!

CHORUS OF WOMEN

    (*To the miners who want to get involved.*)
    Get back! Get back! Stay out of this!
    We don't need you! We can take care of ourselves!

(*The women drive the SHERIFF and DEPUTY back.*)

SHERIFF

    (*The sheriff and his men load their rifles with tear gas and fire the canisters.*) Let's see how you like this! (*The women retreat. Just when it looks like the SHERIFF and his men are about to win, the wind blows the tear gas back into their faces.*)

ALEXANDER

    (*To the SHERIFF.*) Scatter like quail, will they!

DEPUTY

    Let's go, let's go, let's get out now. We didn't sign up to fight women! Let's go! (*They make a tactical retreat, coughing and choking.*)

CHORUS

    (*Cheering.*)
    Chiquiti bim bom ba,
    A la bim bom ba! A la bio, a la bao,
    A la bim bom ba,
    La unión, la unión,
    ¡Ganará!

(*Exit miners and wives, chanting.*)

RAMÓN

Are you all right?

ESPERANZA

Sure! (*Reaching out for the baby*) Here, I'll take him.

ESTELA

Papi, did you see the way Mami knocked the deputy down?

RAMÓN

That was something! I bet you're ready to come home, eh?

ESPERANZA

Nope, I'm staying right here!

ESTELA

Mami, I'm hungry!

ESPERANZA

Ramón, take her home and feed her, will you?

RAMÓN

But she doesn't like my cooking! (*Beat.*) And neither do I! (*Resigned, RAMÓN and ESTELA exit, followed by ESPERANZA. Meanwhile, on another part of the stage, the SHERIFF and ALEXANDER plot their next move.*)

SHERIFF

(*To ALEXANDER.*) So, what do you want me to do now, shoot them down?

ALEXANDER

Have you tried locking them up?

SHERIFF

You want them *all* arrested?

ALEXANDER

No, just the ringleaders, the fire-eaters,
And the ones with big families. Where's that boy, Salvador?

(*The women continue picketing in the background.*)

SHERIFF

(*Enter SALVADOR RUIZ.*) Hey, Pancho, come here! (*The SHERIFF takes out a bullhorn.*)
Awright, girls! I'm gonna give you a choice. You can go home, or you can go to jail.

Get off the picket line or get arrested. (*No answer from the women,
he motions to SALVADOR.*) All right, point 'em out!

SALVADOR

(*Pointing them out.*) That one—Teresa Vidal, she's the leader. (*The
DEPUTY arrests her.*) And Mrs. Salazar, the older one, her husband
was killed in a strike years ago. (*She is arrested.*) And Jesusita, the
militant. (*She is arrested.*) And don't forget Lola Álvarez, the pretty
one. (*She is arrested.*) And Ramón's wife, with the baby, he don't like
her being here at all!

SHERIFF

The one with the baby?

ALEXANDER

Yes, arrest them, arrest them all! (*ESPERANZA, babe in arms, is
arrested. When ESTELA sees the deputies taking the women away, she
runs after them.*)

WOMEN

¡Mujeres, unidas, jamás serán vencidas!
The women, united, will never be divided! (*Repeat.*)

*The SHERIFF and his men march the women off to jail, herding them
into cells. There is no room to sit, so they stand.*

WOMEN

¡Queremos comida! ¡Queremos camas! ¡Queremos leche! ¡Queremos
baños! (*Repeat.*)
¡Las mujeres de Zinc Town pedimos pan, no nos dan!
¡Pedimos queso, nos dan un hueso, y se nos atora en el pescuezo!
The women of Zinc Town ask for bread, we get a stone!
Ask for cheese, we get a bone, and it sticks in our throats!

SHERIFF

Please! Be quiet! Stop that racket!

WOMEN

¡Las mujeres de la unión, unidas son! ¡Pedimos drenaje, puro chantaje!
¡Pedimos baños, por muchos años de desengaños!
The women of the union, united are!
We ask for sewers, they tried to screw us!
We ask for toilets
And all we got were lies, lies, lies!

SHERIFF

I told you once, I told you twice.
We got no food, we got no bread.
We got no toilets, we got no beds!
So, please, please, please, shut up!

*The women keep singing and making a racket. The SHERIFF turns to ALEXANDER.*

WOMEN

We want food! We want beds! We want milk! We want bread!

SHERIFF

What are we going to do? These dames are driving me crazy!

ALEXANDER

Get the J.P. to swear out peace bonds. Hike the bail high enough to keep them in jail.

SHERIFF

Keep them in jail, are you nuts? I can't feed them out of my own pocket!
When are you going to settle this? What are you after, anyway?

ALEXANDER

(*Enter RAMÓN, who listens in, unseen by the SHERIFF.*)
The company has other mines, you have to see the bigger picture. Once these people get their way, they start demanding more and more.

SHERIFF

(*Suddenly, aware of RAMÓN.*) What the hell do you want?

RAMÓN

I came for my kids.

SHERIFF

Good, get 'em and get out! I got no formula, no baby food!
(*The SHERIFF opens the door of the jail.*)

WOMEN

The baby! Bring out the baby! (*ESPERANZA brings the baby to RAMÓN, and he exits with ESTELA and the baby.*)

MRS. SALAZAR

(*Leading the chants.*)
¡Las mujeres de la unión!

WOMEN

¡Unidas son, unidas son! (*Blackout.*)
¡Las mujeres de la unión,
Unidas son, unidas son!

*The Quintero home. RAMÓN is feeding the baby, ESTELA plays nearby. Enter ESPERANZA.*

RAMÓN

How do you feel? How did you sleep? Four nights away from home!

ESPERANZA

We raised such a fuss, they finally brought cots in. I nearly lost my voice, yelling.

RAMÓN

Did you have to sign a pledge not to go back to the line?

ESPERANZA

No, we wouldn't do it. And the sheriff let us go!

RAMÓN

Look, Esperanza, I just can't do this any more!

ESPERANZA

Woman's work ain't easy, is it Ramón?

*A knock on the door. Enter TERESA, MRS. SALAZAR, and some of the other women. RAMÓN is clearly irritated.*

TERESA

It's all set. We're taking over the picket line again tomorrow. We better get organized.

ESPERANZA

Come on in, come in, sit down. (*The women sit down on the couch, RAMÓN is left standing, without a place to sit.*)

RAMÓN

(*Whispering to ESPERANZA.*) I said we've got to talk now, you and me.

ESPERANZA

Ramón, can't you see I'm in the middle of a meeting?

RAMÓN

Damn it! (*RAMÓN exits, slamming the door behind him.*)

TERESA

What are you going to do about him, Esperanza?

MRS. SALAZAR

What if we talked to him?

ESPERANZA

No, I'll handle it. We have to work it out—the two of us! (*The women go back to planning the picket line. Slow fade.*)

*Back in the cantina, disgruntled miners, RAMÓN included, are drinking. Enter FRANK, all disheveled.*

RAMÓN

Jesus, Frank, what happened to you? (*The men gather around FRANK.*)

FRANK

I was in the house and heard something. I stepped out, saw two guys setting my car on fire! I tried to stop them, but they beat me up. The car's a total wreck.

VICENTE

And last week they shot up the union hall.

RAMÓN

Here Frank, calm down. (*Serving him a drink.*) What do we do now?

VICENTE

I got a friend in the Bureau of Mines, know what he says?
Ain't never gonna open up that mine again.

RAMÓN

How come?

VICENTE

The ore's played out, so help me, the ore's played out.

RAMÓN

That's a lot of bull. It's a rich mine. I know it's a rich mine.

FRANK

I'll drink to that.

RAMÓN

¡Salud!

FRANK

> Helped organize a strike a couple years ago in Arizona
> Where the governor called out the National Guard,
> Had all the strikers arrested and put in boxcars,
> Hauled away and dropped off in the middle of the burning Sonoran Desert.
> They'll steal our jobs, so help me, they'll steal our jobs.

MEN

> They'll steal our jobs, they'll never settle, they'll never settle.
> They'll call in the sheriffs, deputies, lawyers, and politicians.
> Then they will serve us with documents signed by a county judge.
> Never settle, never settle,
> They'll call in the sheriffs, deputies, lawyers, and politicians.
> Then they will steal our jobs,
> They'll roll in the scabs on a fleet of trucks,
> They'll serve us with documents all signed,
> They'll never settle.

RAMÓN

> Maybe it's time to get out the guns and let them do the talking!

VICENTE

> What, are you crazy?

RAMÓN

> What difference does it make now? The strike's no longer our fight.

VICENTE

> What do you mean?

RAMÓN

> The women run it, not us

FRANK

> You've got to look at the bigger picture.

RAMÓN

> Yeah, the bigger picture, we're starving to death, that's the bigger picture.

MEN

> You have to look at the bigger picture, the bigger picture. (*Simultaneous with above.*) Maybe it's time to get out the guns and let them do the talking
> What difference does it make now? The strike's no longer ours.

What difference does it make? The strike's no longer ours.
What difference, what difference?

FRANK

I'm with you guys! What I wouldn't give for some meat on the table.

VICENTE

Let's go hunting tomorrow, what do you say?
If we can't live off the mine, maybe we can live off the land.

FRANK

What do you think, Ramón?

RAMÓN

Why ask me? Am I running this strike?

VICENTE

You'll come?

RAMÓN

Let's go.

VICENTE

I'll drink to that!

MEN

They'll never settle, they'll never settle.
They'll call in the congressmen and serve us with documents,
Signed by a county judge,
Roll in the scabs on a fleet of trucks,
They'll never settle! Time to get out the guns.
(*The men raise their glasses, toast, and drink. Blackout.*)

*Lights up on ESPERANZA, pacing, in the kitchen. Enter RAMÓN.*

ESPERANZA

I waited up till midnight.

RAMÓN

You weren't waiting for me. (*Going to get his rifle.*)

ESPERANZA

My first night home. Why did you leave me?

RAMÓN

You weren't waiting for me.

ESPERANZA

Can't you stand the sight of me?

RAMÓN

Be quiet!

ESPERANZA

What is it? Tell me. Tell me.

RAMÓN

I don't know what to do.

The shopkeepers look at me as if I were a thief.

The priest calls me a Communist from the pulpit of the church.

My own daughter won't follow orders, and you, Esperanza,

I don't know you any more!

(*RAMÓN cleans the rifle with a rag, working the bolt action, adjusting the scope.*)

ESPERANZA

Where are you going with that rifle?

RAMÓN

Hunting.

ESPERANZA

Ramón, we need you here.

RAMÓN

For what? To feed the baby? You can do that.

What's the use, the company can starve us out!

ESPERANZA

They're dying to reopen.

RAMÓN

You don't see the bigger picture.

They'll just wait, six months or nine,

They don't care, they can outlast us,

They don't care if they close the mine.

ESPERANZA

You mean you're ready to give up? You sound like a man defeated!

RAMÓN

I'll not give up. Never! I'd rather die on my feet like a man than live on bended knees.

ESPERANZA

You want to go down fighting? A man defeated?
Noble words! But I don't want to go down. I want to win!
Didn't you learn from the strike?
We are not weaker, we're stronger than before.
Husbands with their wives as partners, now we begin.
Stronger than before.
They thought you wouldn't strike, they were wrong.
They tried to break our line, and they failed.
They beat you, you didn't give up.
They jailed us, we packed the jails.
If we stand together, they won't win.
As long as we stay together!
That's why we need you here, Ramón,
They mean to try something else, something big.

RAMÓN

Like what?

ESPERANZA

I don't know, but I can feel it like the calm before the storm. 'Chente
says . . .

RAMÓN

(*Exploding.*) Vicente says! Don't throw Vicente up to me!

ESPERANZA

'Chente's our compadre, Ramón. Are you jealous of him?
Why are you afraid of me? To have me by your side?
Can you have dignity, only if I have none?

RAMÓN

What are you talking about?

ESPERANZA

Respect, Ramón. I talk of dignity.
Dignidad es todo lo que quiero.
The bosses exploit you, some Anglos look down on you.
The message they say is, "Stay in your place, you dirty Mexican."
So, why do you say to me, "Stay in your place!"

RAMÓN

You're talking crazy!

ESPERANZA

>    Whose neck shall I step on? Whose neck to make me feel strong and
>    superior?
>    I was so low, as low as could be, but I want to rise
>    And push everything with me as I grow. Can't you see?
>    ¡Que somos iguales! Tú y yo, nosotros.

RAMÓN

>    Shut up, I said!

ESPERANZA

>    If you can't see this—you're a fool! (*RAMÓN almost slaps her.*)
>    That would be the old way. Don't try that again—never!
>    I am going to bed now. Sleep where you can, but not with me!
>    (*ESPERANZA exits, leaving RAMÓN alone in the dark.*)

*The action in this final scene takes place simultaneously on three fronts.
Enter ALEXANDER and the SHERIFF, followed by two deputies.*

SHERIFF

>    A group of men went hunting early this morning.

ALEXANDER

>    And the women?

SHERIFF

>    At the picket line.

ALEXANDER

>    OK. Now's the time! (*They exit.*)

*Enter VICENTE, thinking he has spotted a deer. He hears something and
points his rifle as if to shoot. Enter RAMÓN. VICENTE puts down his
rifle.*

VICENTE

>    (*Angry and frustrated.*) Damn it, Ramón! I almost shot you!

RAMÓN

>    Sorry, Vicente, my mind isn't in this.

VINCENTE

>    What the hell's wrong with you? You've been in a daze all morning.

RAMÓN

>    Something Esperanza said rings true.
>    She has a way of speaking I can't ignore,

Try as I might, I know she's right,
Her words strike me to the very core.
I can't deny it, can't hide it,
She's my conscience, my other self,
A small voice I can't ignore,
Her words strike me to the very core.
(*Turning suddenly to VICENTE.*)
Vicente, we got to go back now!

VICENTE

What are you talking about, we haven't bagged a single deer!

RAMÓN

Never mind. I'll explain later. Let's go, the women need us. (*They exit.*)

*At the picket line, the women are huddled together, dispirited and shivering, hunched against the biting wind. We never lose focus or sight of them.*

TERESA

So, they had a little taste of what it's like to be a woman.

MRS. SALAZAR

Ran away to go deer hunting. Deserters!

ESPERANZA

I struck at his pride, spoke out of bitterness, this hurt him.

ALEXANDER

(*Entering the shantytown with the SHERIFF and his deputies.*)
Evict the Quinteros first and let their neighbors watch. Then we'll throw the others out.
(*A deputy enters the Quintero house.*)

MRS. SALAZAR

(*Noticing the activity.*) Esperanza, the sheriff is at your house! (*The women run to the shantytown.*)

SHERIFF

(*The women gather around, watching the deputies take out furniture from the Quintero household.*)
All right, girls—get back, get back! This is company property.
They got an eviction notice, perfectly within their rights.

TERESA

We can't let them throw you out into the street like that!

SHERIFF

There's nothing, nothing you can do.

(*ESTELA picks up some dirt clods and throws them at the deputies. One of them tries to catch her.*) Never mind that brat! Move this junk out!

VICENTE

(*Enter with RAMÓN.*) ¡Hijos de puta! ¡Cabrones! (*VICENTE raises the barrel of his rifle as if to shoot.*)

RAMÓN

(*Taking the rifle away from VICENTE and giving it to a startled MRS. SALAZAR.*) Vicente! We're not going to go down fighting, we're going to win! We can do it, Esperanza! This is the moment we've been waiting for!

ESPERANZA

What do you mean?

RAMÓN

They're trying to evict us! They've given up trying to break the picket line.

The only way they can win is by throwing us out of the company town.

ESPERANZA

Now we can fight them, all of us, together!

*RAMÓN whispers in ESPERANZA's ear. She reacts and tells the other women. The deputies take out the furniture from the front, but the women pick the furniture back up and bring it into the house via the back.*

SHERIFF

(*Frustrated.*) Hey! Stop it! You can't do that!

MRS. SALAZAR

Oh yeah, just watch us!

DEPUTY

(*Struggling with two women.*) Let go of that furniture! (*The women yank it away from him.*)

SHERIFF

Damn it all to hell! (*The women laugh.*) See here, Quintero! These women are obstructing justice! You make 'em behave, savvy?

RAMÓN

Sorry sheriff, I can't do nothing. You know how it is—they won't listen to a man no more!

SHERIFF

You want me to lock them up again?

RAMÓN

You want them in your lockup again? (*The SHERIFF and his men stop, as the women move the furniture back into the Quintero home.*)

TERESA

We stopped them, we stopped them!

VICENTE

Way to go, gals!

FRANK

It took all we had, but we stopped them!

JESUSITA

Did you see the look on their faces? Did you see?

LOLA

I knew we could do it, I knew it!

MRS. SALAZAR

This is just the first battle, Lola, we haven't won the war yet.

SHERIFF

(*To ALEXANDER.*) Got any more bright ideas, chief?

ALEXANDER

(*Furious.*) Arrest that son of a bitch Quintero! Can't you see he's behind this?

SHERIFF

And have another riot on my hands?

RAMÓN

(*Embracing ESPERANZA.*)
¡Gracias, Esperanza, mil gracias!

ESPERANZA

For what?

RAMÓN

For showing me the way.

RAMÓN/ESPERANZA

When I spoke, you listened.
When I felt despair, you give me hope,
When I wanted to quit, you stood fast,
When I hurt you, you forgave me.

SHERIFF

(*To ALEXANDER.*) Listen here, you stupid Yankee, I have to live
with these people! You don't!

ALEXANDER

All right, calm down, I'll call New York. We'll settle. For now, for
now.

RAMÓN

I can go back to work and provide for us.

ESPERANZA

We'll provide together, you and I.

ESPERANZA/ RAMÓN

This land, our land, New Mexico!

ALL

New Mexico, give up your veins of silver.
New Mexico, enchantress,
Give up the veins of gold
That lie within your mountains.
Nuevo México, encantadora,
No nos engañes, dame el oro
De tu tierra amarilla.
Algún día tu plata será mía.
Share your riches with us,
Land of our birth.
With your children of the sun,
The salt of the earth.

## The End